Reverse Engineering Embedded ARM Binaries

By Example

By Yury Magda

The programs, examples, and applications presented in this book have been included for their instructional value. The author offers no warranty implied or express, including but not limited to implied warranties of fitness or merchantability for any particular purpose and do not accept any liability for any loss or damage arising from the use of any information in this book, or any error or omission in such information, or any incorrect use of these programs, procedures, and applications.

To my wife, Julia

About the Author

Yury Magda is an embedded engineer experienced in designing hardware and software for Intel x86- and ARM-based systems. He is also the author of the books on designing embedded systems based upon various development platforms.

Introduction

This book is thought as a highly practical guide to reverse engineering embedded ARM binaries. There may be various reasons why we need to reverse a binary running on some embedded system. In practice, reversing ARM binaries may be necessary when we want to adjust some existing embedded system to new or updated conditions, but we don't have a source code to completely rebuild an embedded application.
This guide illustrates various approaches that can be applied while reversing ARM binaries. The reverse engineering techniques are illustrated in the demo examples based upon the real-life designs using the STM32F7 and ATSAMD21 microcontrollers. Analyzing binaries is implemented using GHIDRA 9.2.2 that is a freely available open source SRE tool suite from the National Security Agency (NSA).

Disclaimer

While the author has used good faith efforts to ensure that the information and instructions contained in this book are accurate, the author disclaims all responsibility for errors or omissions, including without limitation responsibility for damages resulting from the use of or reliance on this work. Use of the information and instructions contained in this work is at your own risk. If any code samples or other technology this book contains or describes is subject to open source licenses or the intellectual property rights of others, it is your responsibility to ensure that your use thereof complies with such licenses and/or rights. All example applications from this book were developed and tested without damaging hardware. The author will not accept any responsibility for damages of any kind due to actions taken by you after reading this book.

Basic Usage of GHIDRA

To reverse embedded ARM binaries, we will use the free and easy to use GHIDRA Disassembler/Decompiler tool that provides great capabilities for both reverse engineers and experienced developers (**Fig.1**).

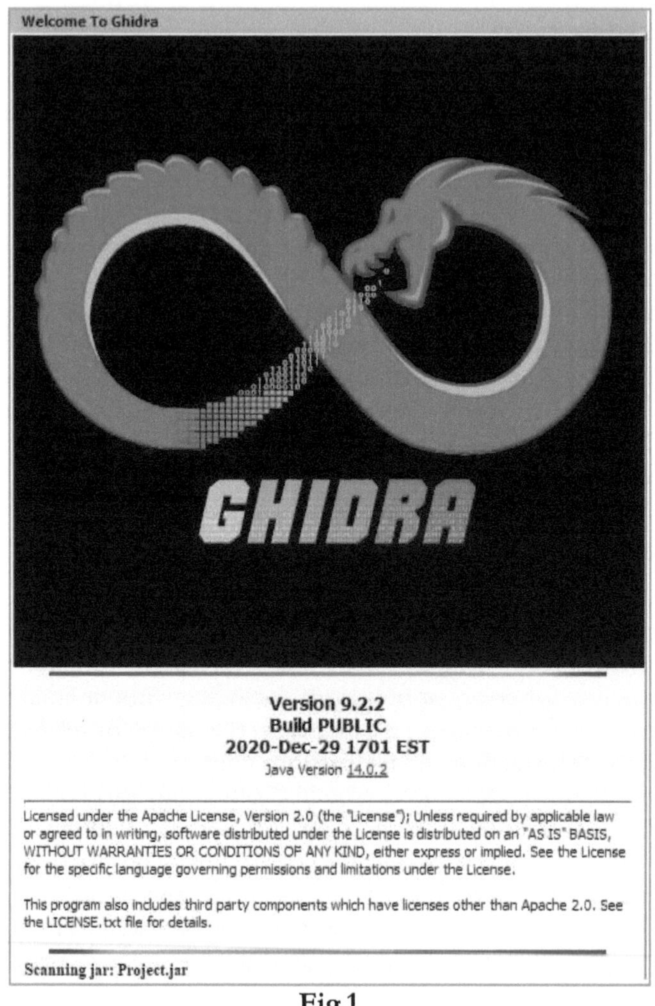

Fig.1

GHIDRA is a great tool for performing reverse engineering embedded binaries. This tool is built upon a completely generic application framework with the additional capabilities provided by small software bundles ("plugins"). The GHIDRA's reverse engineering capabilities are described in detail in the user's guide. The complete information about GHIDRA can be found on the Help page or by surfing https://ghidra-sre.org.

The following simplified sequence can be applied while reversing an embedded ARM binary:

1. Examine how the existing embedded system is running;
2. Consider the ways for modifying the embedded code in order to get the desired result;
3. Identify the microcontroller (MCU) installed on a target board and find the maximum information about this device (datasheet(s), programming and reference manuals, etc.) to ease your task;
4. Get an existing ARM binary (HEX file);
5. Determine the tools (programmers and/or debuggers) that can be used to download the patched binary into the MCU flash memory. There is no reason to continue the job if you can't download the patched executable into an embedded system;
6. Import a binary file into GHIDRA and analyze the code;
7. Choose the suitable scenario of patching the binary;
8. Patch an existing binary and export the patched code into an Intel HEX file;
9. Download the patched HEX file into the MCU flash memory.

This sequence is very simplified. In real life, the procedure may be much more complicated. Let's go to practical examples of reversing embedded ARM binaries.

Example 1

An existing embedded system based upon the STM32F722 microcontroller (MCU) produces a PWM signal on pin **PE9** that feeds some external circuitry (**Fig.2**).

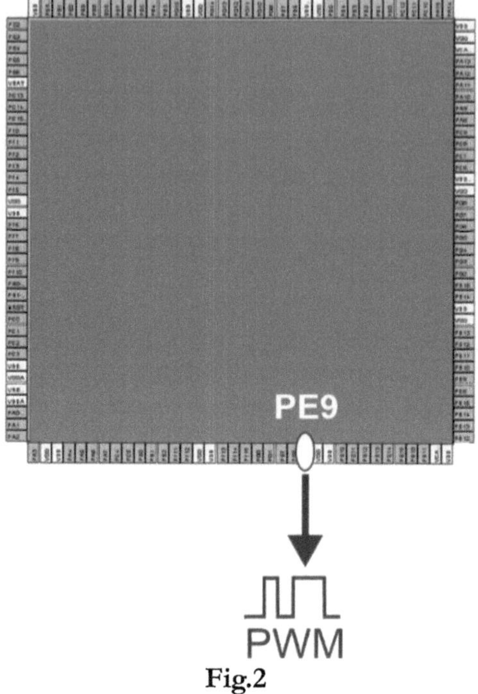

Fig.2

We need to update the embedded code so that PWM will be disabled when the positive-going signal from a touch sensor arrives on some pin of MCU (**Fig.3**).

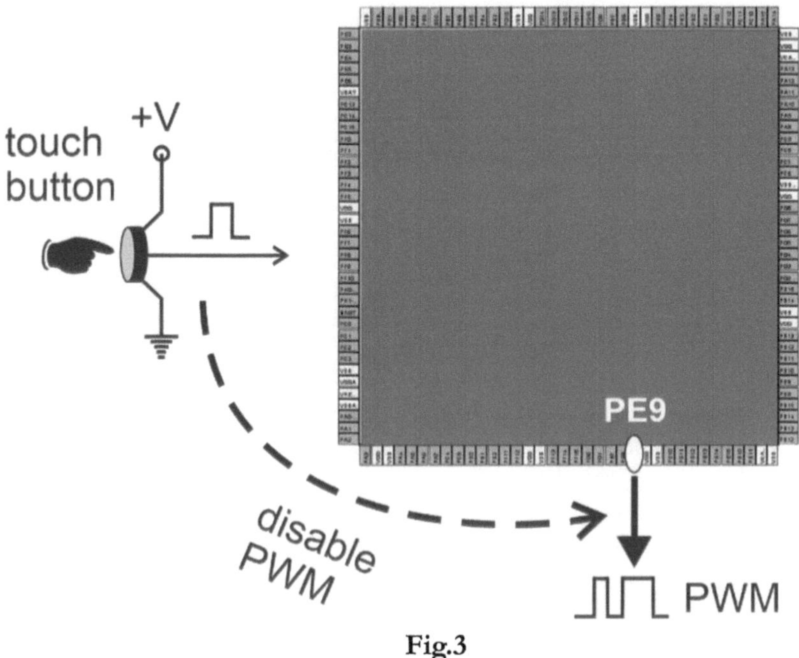

Fig.3

Before patching the existing system, we must determine what free I/O pin to use for attaching the touch sensor.
We also need to determine what peripheral device produces a PWM signal on pin **PE9**. Usually, PWM is produced by some timer. In our particular case, the best candidate is Timer 1 whose Channel 1 uses pin **PE9** as output. Therefore, our task becomes clearer - to disable the signal of the Channel 1 of Timer 1 when the signal from a touch sensor arrives.
At the next step, we will analyze the HEX file.

Analyzing a binary

To analyze the existing binary (HEX file), we launch the GHIDRA Disassembler and create a new project (named **demo1_patch**, **Fig.4** - **Fig.5**).

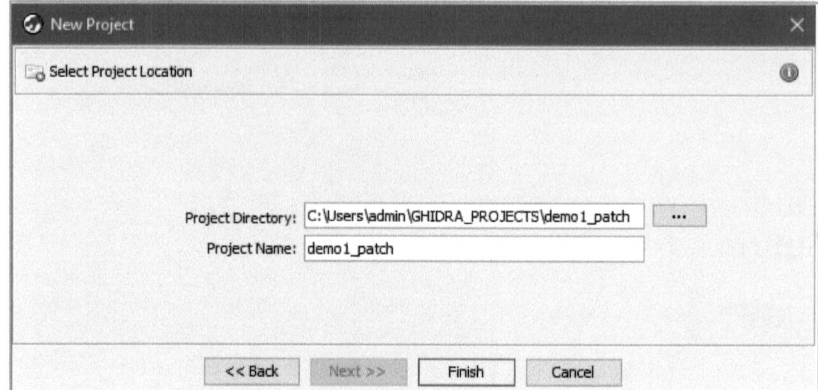

Fig.4

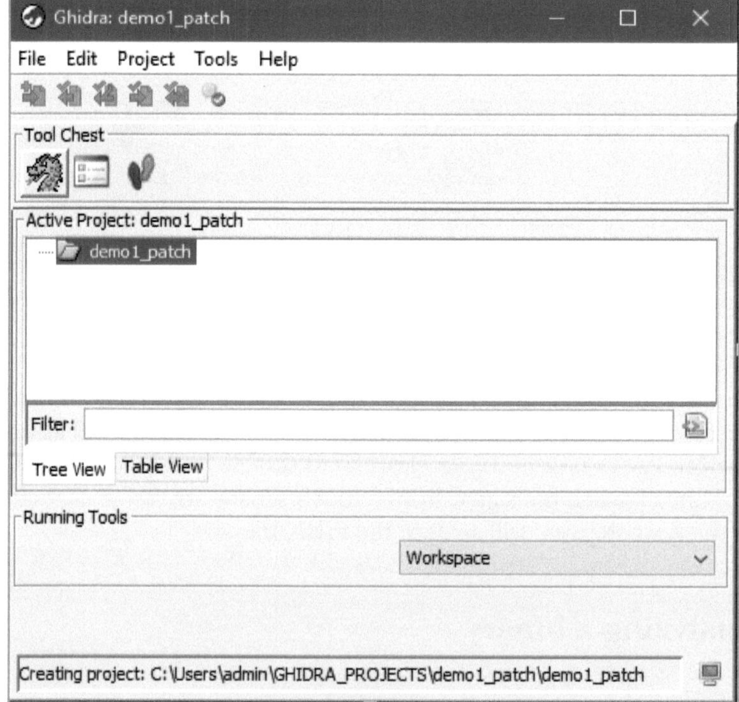

Fig.5

Then we add the existing HEX file to the project using the **File→Import File…** option (**Fig.6** - **Fig.7**).

Ghidra: demo1_patch
File
Edit
Project
Tools
Help
New Project... Ctrl+N
Open Project... Ctrl+O
Reopen
Close Project Ctrl+W
Save Project Ctrl+S
Delete Project...
Archive Current Project...
Restore Project...
Configure...
Install Extensions...
Import File... I
Batch Import...
Open File System... Ctrl+I
Exit Ghidra Ctrl+Q
Workspace
Creating project: C:\Users\admin\GHIDRA_PROJECTS\demo1_patch\demo1_patch

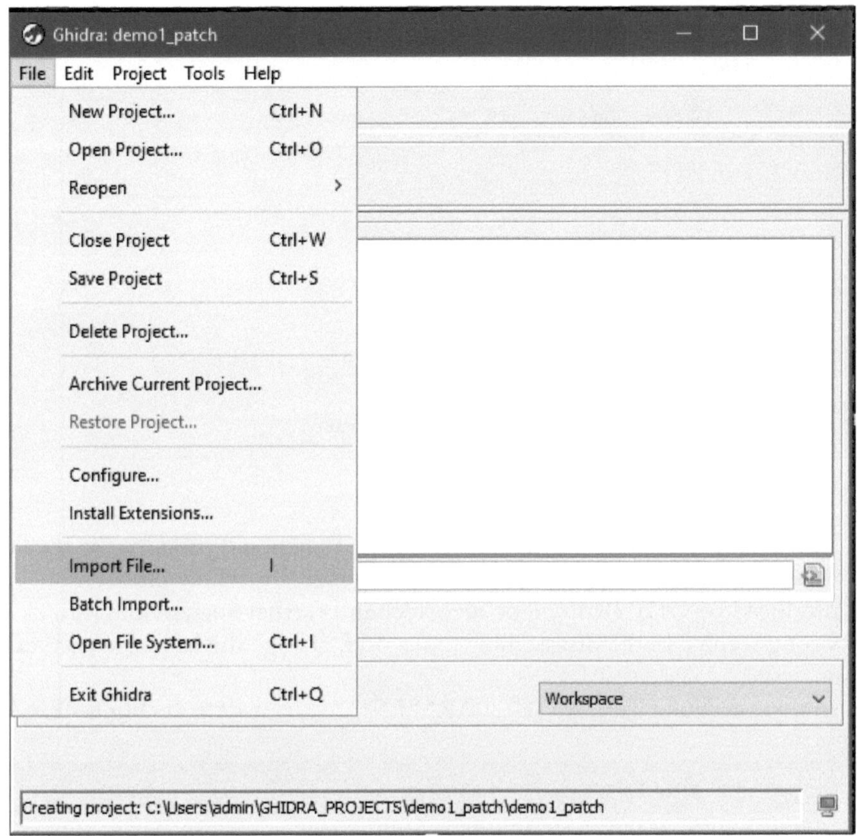

Fig.6

Import /G:/Rev_Bin/demo1.hex

Format: Intel Hex
Language:
Destination Folder: demo1_patch:/
Program Name: demo1.hex
Options...
Please select a language.
OK Cancel

Fig.7

At this stage, we should select the language that would produce the quality disassembly. If we select the incorrect language, the whole disassembly produced by GHIDRA will be incorrect and further analysis can lead us to wrong results. If the disassembly looks odd, change the language and repeat analysis.

In this particular case, we select ARM:LE:32:Cortex:default (**Fig.8** - **Fig.9**).

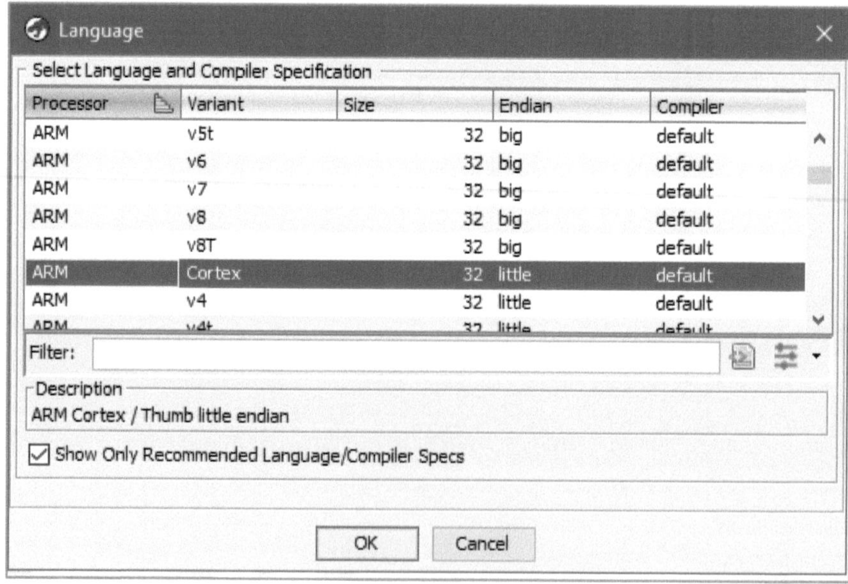

Fig.8

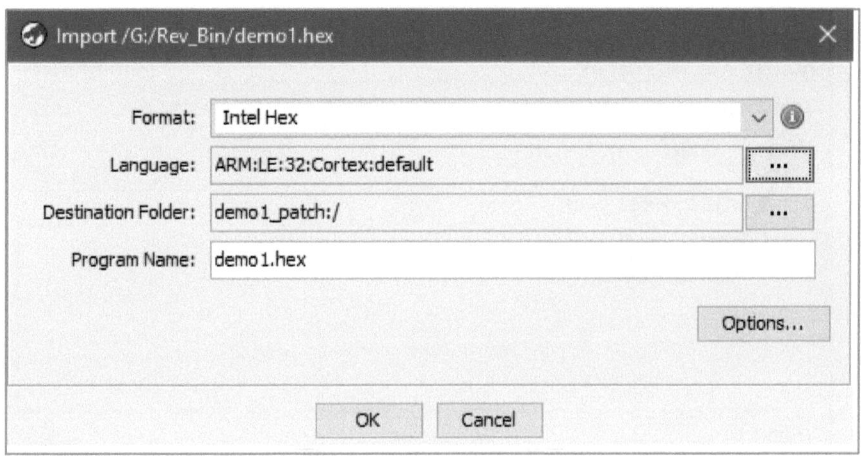

Fig.9

When we are done, simply drag the **demo1.hex** to **CodeBrowser** (**Fig.10**).

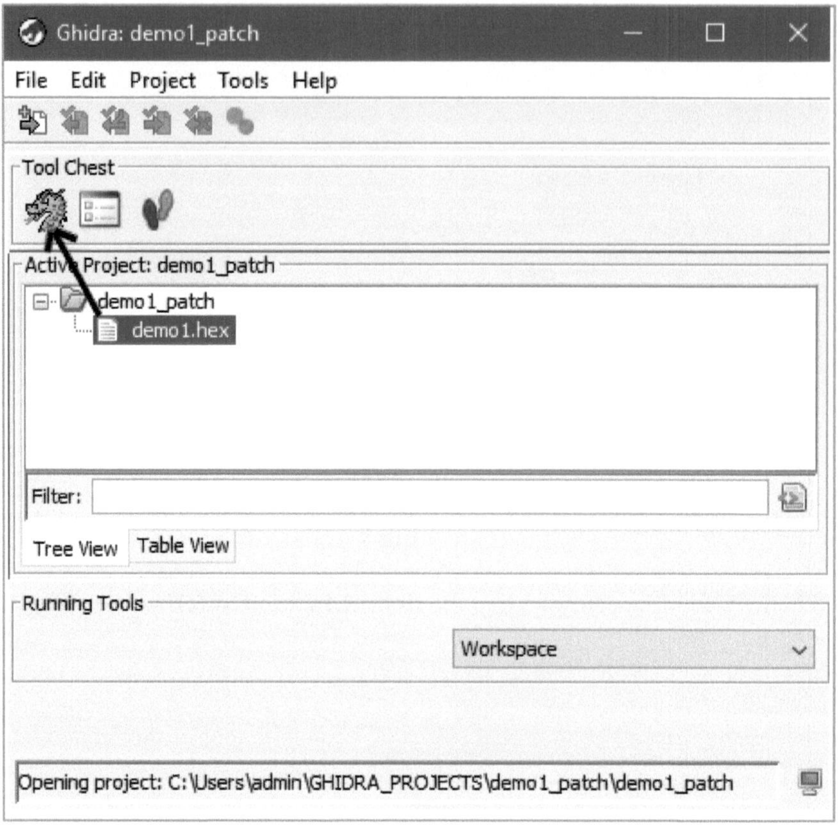

Fig.10

Then the **CodeBrowser** window opens and we are prompted to analyze the HEX file (**Fig.11**).

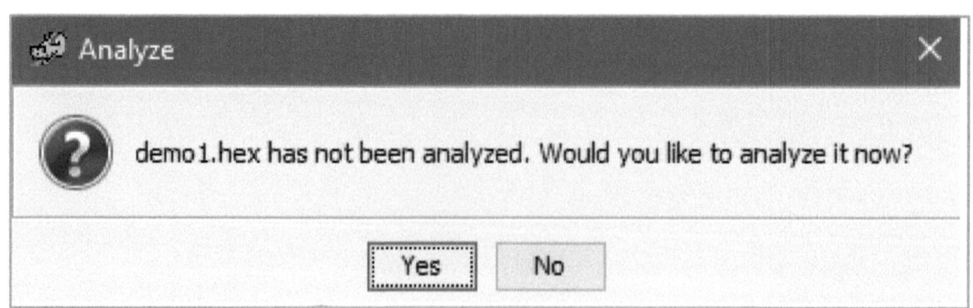

Fig.11

After clicking **Yes**, the **Analysis Options** window appears (**Fig.12**).

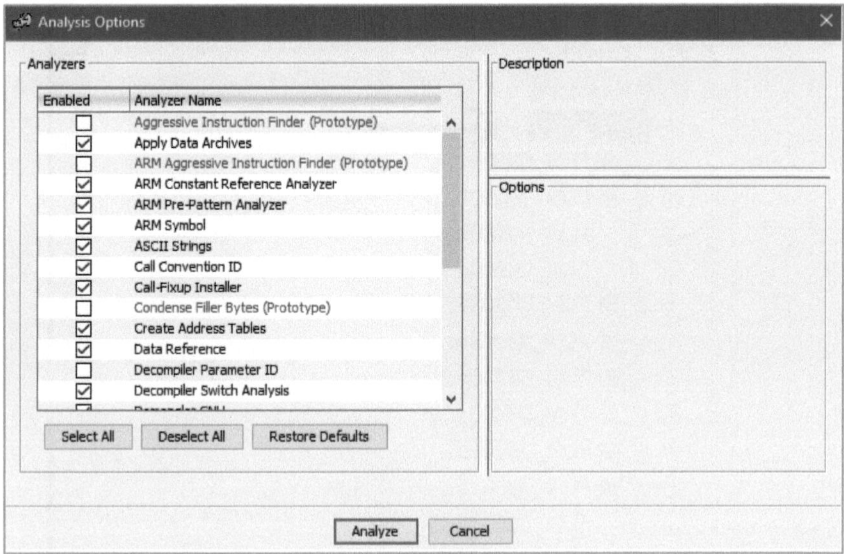

Fig.12

In this case, we will not change the default settings, therefore click **Analyze** and wait until analyzing is complete.
Then from the disassembly, we will determine the **entry** point that will lead us to the **main()** function code. This helps us to better understand the structure of disassembly and simplify the further analysis.

After we begin to search for the **entry** point, we can view the results in the **Symbol Tree** window (**Fig.13**).

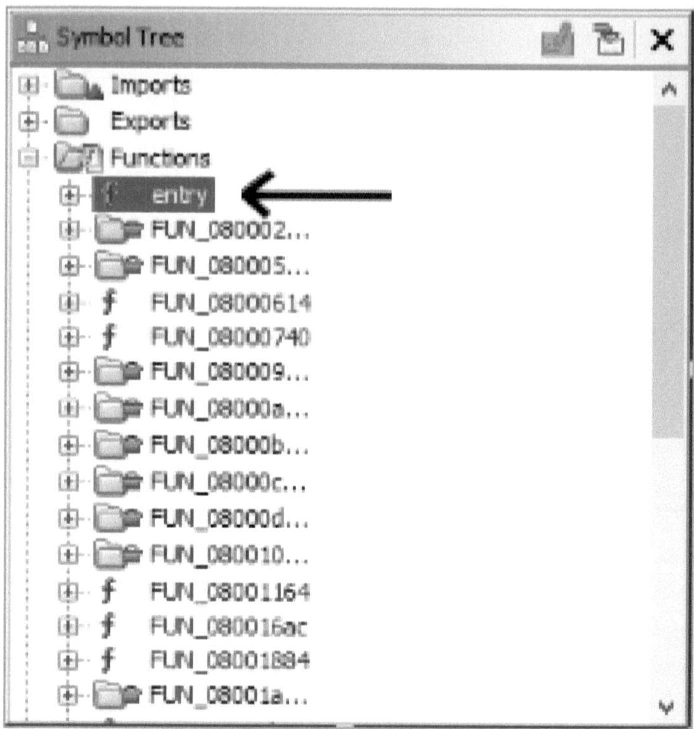

Fig.13

The fragment of disassembly corresponding to **entry()** is shown in **Listing** (**Fig.14**) and **Decompile** (**Fig.15**) windows.

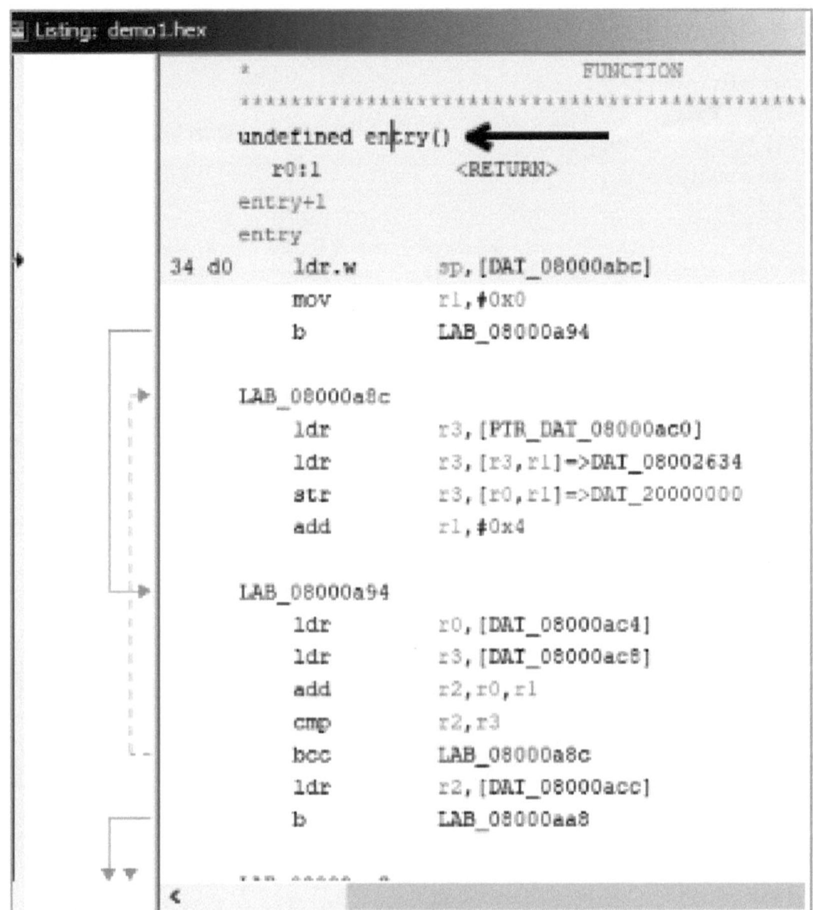

Fig.14

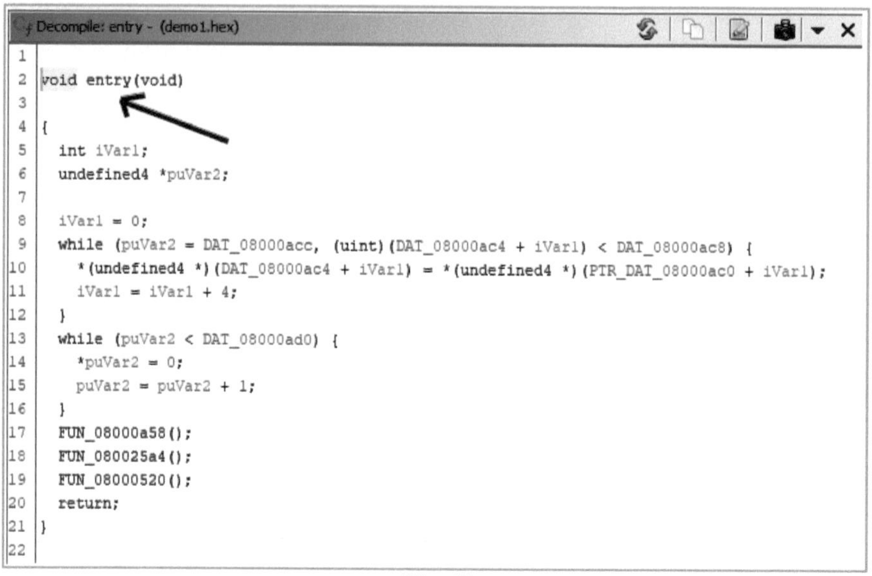

```
Decompile: entry - (demo1.hex)

void entry(void)

{
  int iVar1;
  undefined4 *puVar2;

  iVar1 = 0;
  while (puVar2 = DAT_08000acc, (uint)(DAT_08000ac4 + iVar1) < DAT_08000ac8) {
    *(undefined4 *)(DAT_08000ac4 + iVar1) = *(undefined4 *)(PTR_DAT_08000ac0 + iVar1);
    iVar1 = iVar1 + 4;
  }
  while (puVar2 < DAT_08000ad0) {
    *puVar2 = 0;
    puVar2 = puVar2 + 1;
  }
  FUN_08000a58();
  FUN_080025a4();
  FUN_08000520();
  return;
}
```

Fig.15

Usually, the **main()** code is located near the **entry** point, therefore in order to find **main()**, we can carefully examine the **entry()** function presented in the **Decompile** window (**Listing 1**).

Listing 1.

```
void entry(void)
{
 int iVar1;
 undefined4 *puVar2;

 iVar1 = 0;
 while (puVar2 = DAT_08000acc, (uint)(DAT_08000ac4 + iVar1) <
DAT_08000ac8) {
   *(undefined4 *)(DAT_08000ac4 + iVar1) = *(undefined4
*)(PTR_DAT_08000ac0 + iVar1);
   iVar1 = iVar1 + 4;
 }
 while (puVar2 < DAT_08000ad0) {
   *puVar2 = 0;
```

```
    puVar2 = puVar2 + 1;
  }
  FUN_08000a58();
  FUN_080025a4();
  FUN_08000520();
  return;
}
```

In embedded systems, the **main()** function usually enters an endless **while()** of **for()** loop, therefore the **main()** code doesn't return. For that reason, no code that goes after a non-returning function will be executed. Looking at the above code, we can assume that the best candidate for the **main()** function is **FUN_08000520()**.
Double-clicking on **FUN_08000520()** in the **Decompile** window brings us to the next window (**Fig.16**).

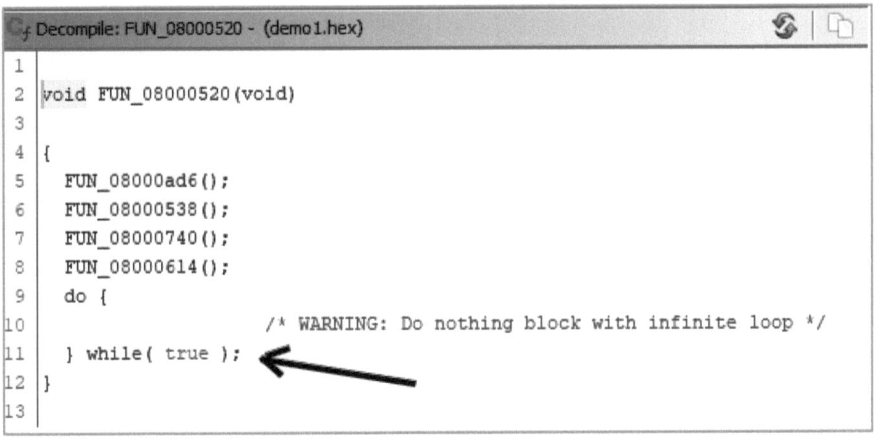

Decompile: FUN_08000520 - (demo1.hex)

```

void FUN_08000520(void)

{
  FUN_08000ad6();
  FUN_08000538();
  FUN_08000740();
  FUN_08000614();
  do {
                    /* WARNING: Do nothing block with infinite loop */
  } while( true );
}

```

Fig.16

The code within function **FUN_08000520()** is shown in **Listing 2.**

Listing 2.

```
void FUN_08000520(void)
{
  FUN_08000ad6();
  FUN_08000538();
```

```
  FUN_08000740();
  FUN_08000614();
  do {
          /* WARNING: Do nothing block with infinite loop */
  } while( true );
}
```

It seems reasonable to assume that the sequence of functions in this code implement some initialization steps before the endless **do…while** loop is entered. For convenience, rename function **FUN_08000520** to **main**. **Note** that there may also be other candidates for **main()**. Further traversing the disassembly gives us the following (**Listing 3)**.

Listing 3.

```
void FUN_08000904(void)
{
  disableIRQinterrupts();
  do {
              /* WARNING: Do nothing block with infinite loop */
  } while( true );
}
```

Here function **FUN_08000904** while running also enters an endless **while()** loop, but the statement

disableIRQinterrupts();

hints that the processor interrupts will be disabled after this function has been executed. In fact, the application will be stopped. Such a code is common for exception handlers; therefore, we can skip over this function.

Once we have the disassembly of **main()**, we can think about placing a patch within this function. Recall that we need to modify the ARM code so that to disable PWM on the Timer 1 Channel 1 output while pin **PA6** goes HIGH. The disassembly of the **main()** function gives us the following (**Listing 4**).

Listing 4.

```
***************************************************
*                    FUNCTION                     *
***************************************************
            undefined main(void)
 undefined       r0:1         <RETURN>
                      main                  XREF[1]: entry:08000ab6(c)
08000520 80 b5          push    { r7, lr }
08000522 00 af          add     r7, sp, #0x0
08000524 00 f0 d7 fa    bl      FUN_08000ad6
08000528 00 f0 06 f8    bl      FUN_08000538
0800052c 00 f0 08 f9    bl      FUN_08000740
08000530 00 f0 70 f8    bl      FUN_08000614

                  LAB_08000534
08000534 fe e7          b       LAB_08000534
08000536 00             ??      00h
08000537 00             ??      00h
```

As we can see, a **do...while()** endless loop in **main()** is implemented through a branch instruction

```
08000534 fe e7          b       LAB_08000534
```

It is also seen that no additional instructions are placed within this loop. We can't insert a patch into this loop, because there is no enough space for placing additional instructions. One possible way to overcome this limitation is to place the patch in an additional memory block as is illustrated in **Fig.17**.

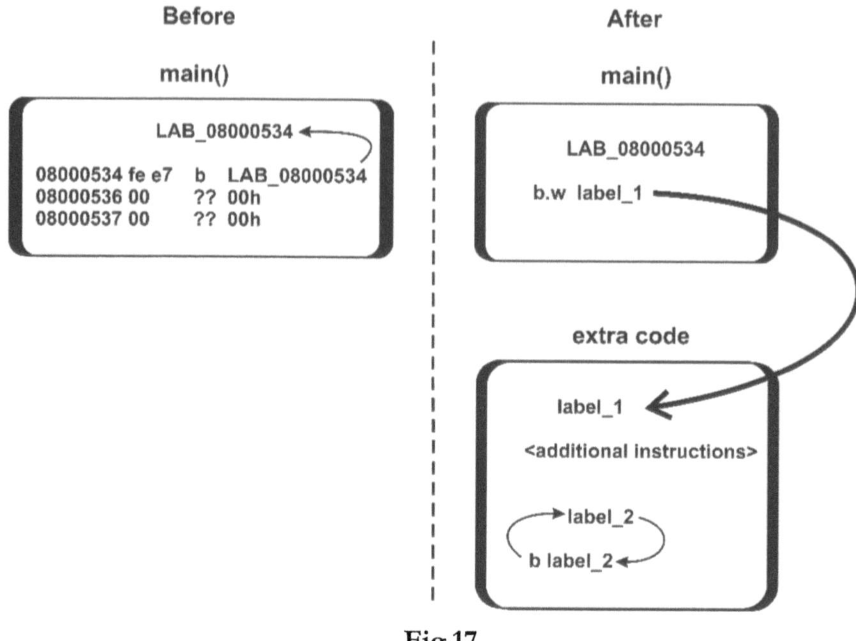

Fig.17

This includes a few steps to perform:

1. allocate enough space for placing a patch (**extra code**);
2. place a patch (**additional instructions**) whose last instruction is

   ```
   b label_2
   ```

   This instruction will implement the new endless loop.
3. to reach the patch code, replace the existing branch instruction

   ```
   b LAB_08000534
   ```

   with

   ```
   b.w label_1
   ```

This will allow to pass control to the patch located at **label_1**.
The next section shows in detail how to write the patch.

Patching a HEX file

First, we should allocate some space for creating an extra code. To do that, click on the **Display Memory Map** icon (**Fig.18**) in the **CodeBrowser** window.

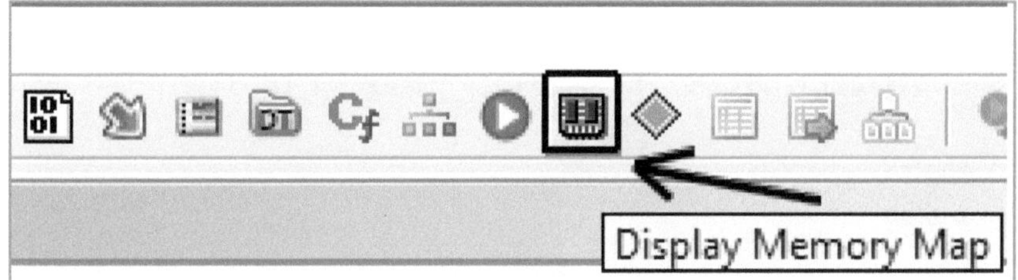

Fig.18

In the next window click "+" (**Fig.19**) in order to add a new block to memory.

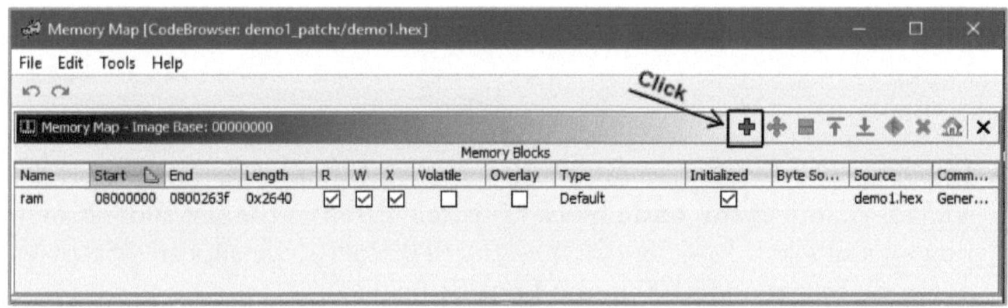

Fig.19

In the **Add Memory Block** dialog box, we should type the values as is shown in **Fig.20**.

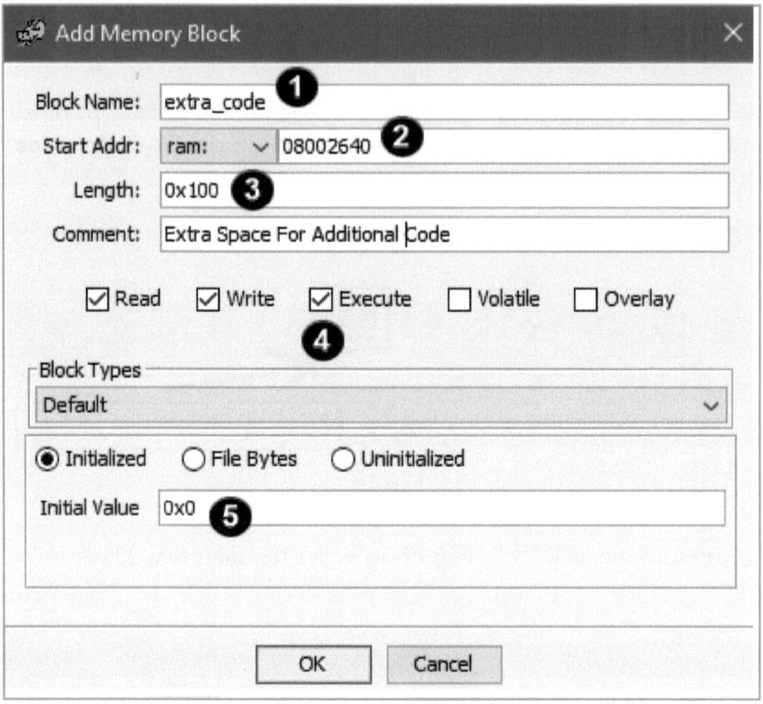

Add Memory Block

Block Name: extra_code
Start Addr: ram: 08002640
Length: 0x100
Comment: Extra Space For Additional Code

Read Write Execute Volatile Overlay

Block Types
Default

Initialized File Bytes Uninitialized

Initial Value 0x0

OK Cancel

Fig.20

In our case, the new memory block is named **extra_code** (**1**). The start address of the **extra_code** block (**2**) is calculated as the last address of the previous block + 1 (= 0800263f + 1 = 08002640). We allocate 256 bytes for our code by typing 0x100 in the **Length** field (**3**).
We also need to check **Execute** (4) and initialize the memory block with 0x0 (**5**). Finally, we get the following (**Fig.21**).

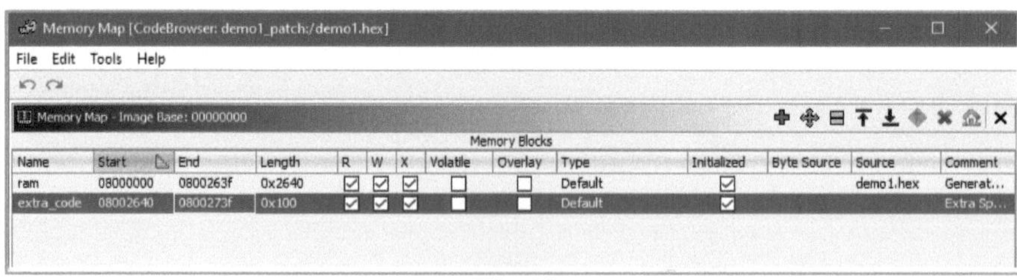

Fig.21

Save the changes and begin to develop the patch that will be placed in the **extra_code** block.

Our patch must operate with GPIO pin **PA6** and Timer 1, therefore we need to access these peripherals through their memory-mapped registers.
Let's define the addresses of these memory-mapped registers.
First, place the 4-byte base address of port GPIOA at the first address (08002640) of the **extra_code** memory block (**Fig.22**).

```
0800263e 00          ??          00h
0800263f 00          ??          00h
                     //
                     // extra_code
                     // Extra Space For Additional Code
                     // ram:08002640-ram:0800273f
                     //
08002640 00          ??          00h
08002641 00          ??          00h
08002642 00          ??          00h
08002643 00          ??          00h
08002644 00          ??          00h
08002645 00          ??          00h
08002646 00          ??          00h
```

Fig.22

Right-click on this address and select **Data→Choose Data Type…** (**Fig.23**).

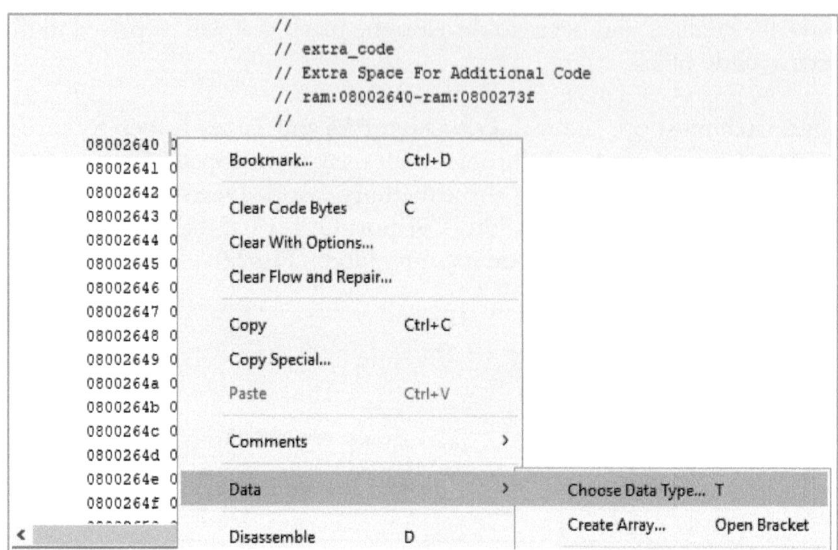

Fig.23

Then in the opened window select the type **undefined4** (**Fig.24**).

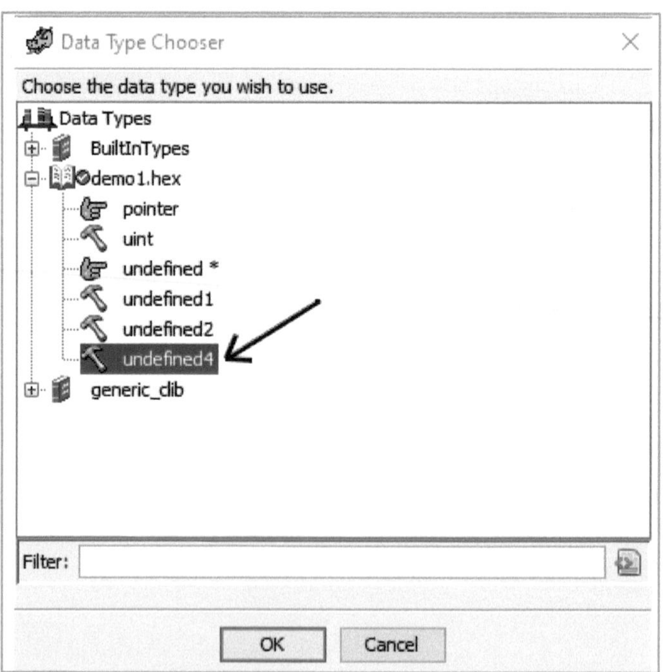

Fig.24

Assign the label **gpioa_base** to this data by choosing **Add Label…** (**Fig.25** - **Fig.26**).

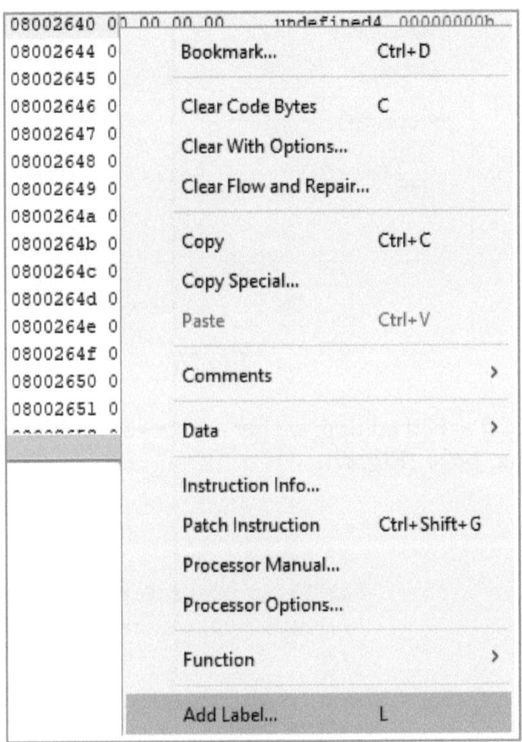

Fig.25

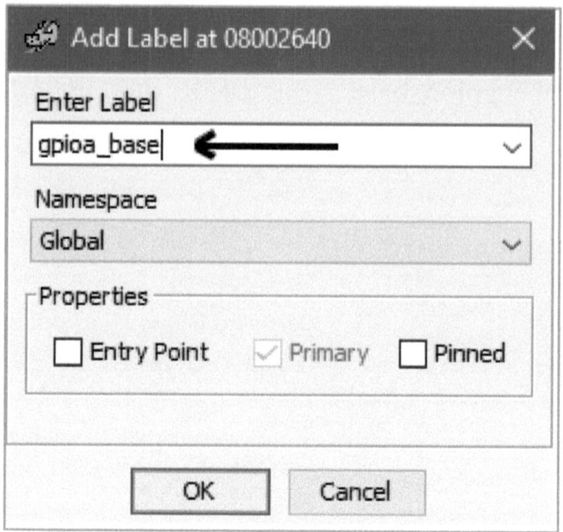

Fig.26

When we are finished editing, we get 4-byte zero-initialized memory block labeled **gpioa_base** (**Fig.27**).

```
                        //
                        // extra_code
                        // Extra Space For Additional Code
                        // ram:08002640-ram:0800273f
                        //

                        gpioa_base
08002640 00 00 00 00       undefined4  00000000h
08002644 00                ??          00h
08002645 00                ??          00h
```

Fig.27

The base address of port GPIOA of STM32F722 MCU is 0x40020000. We need to initialize **gpioa_base** with this value in order to access pin **PA6.** To do that, place the cursor at the address 08002640 and click on the **Display Bytes** icon (**Fig.28**).

Fig.28

Then in the opened window enable editing bytes (**Fig.29**) and update 4 bytes beginning from address 08002640 (**Fig.30**).

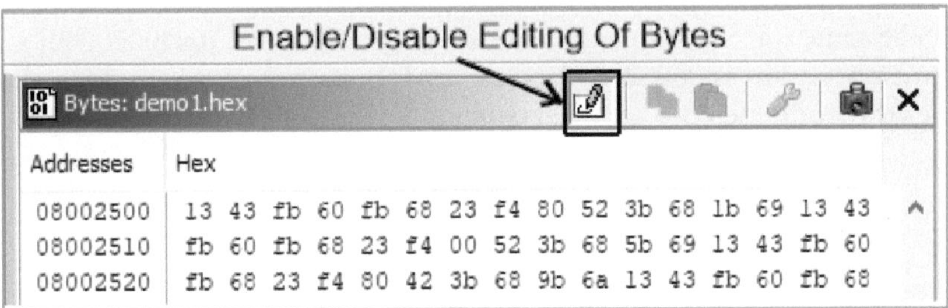

Addresses	Hex															
08002500	13	43	fb	60	fb	68	23	f4	80	52	3b	68	1b	69	13	43
08002510	fb	60	fb	68	23	f4	00	52	3b	68	5b	69	13	43	fb	60
08002520	fb	68	23	f4	80	42	3b	68	9b	6a	13	43	fb	60	fb	68

Fig.29

Bytes: demo1.hex

Addresses	Hex															
080025e0	2c	26	00	08	2c	26	00	08	30	26	00	08	02	44	03	46
080025f0	93	42	00	d1	70	47	03	f8	01	1b	f9	e7	f8	b5	00	bf
08002600	f8	bc	08	bc	9e	46	70	47	f8	b5	00	bf	f8	bc	08	bc
08002610	9e	46	70	47	00	00	00	00	00	00	00	00	01	02	03	04
08002620	06	07	08	09	2c	dc	ff	7f	01	00	00	00	05	02	00	08
08002630	e1	01	00	08	00	24	f4	00	10	00	00	00	01	00	00	00
....	..	..	..	..	..	..	..	..	..	..	..	..	..	..	..	..
08002640	00	00	02	40	00	00	00	00	00	00	00	00	00	00	00	00
08002650	00	00	00	00	00	00	00	00	00	00	00	00	00	00	00	00

Fig.30

After saving changes, the **gpioa_base** memory block will look like the following (**Fig.31**):

```
                    //
                    // extra_code
                    // Extra Space For Additional Code
                    // ram:08002640-ram:0800273f
                    //

                    gpioa_base
08002640 00 00 02 40     undefined4  40020000h
08002644 00              ??          00h
08002645 00              ??          00h
```

Fig.31

The same way we define the base address of Timer 1 (0x40010000) at the memory address 08002644 labeled **tim1_base**. When we are done, the **extra_code** memory area will contain the following (**Fig.32**):

```
                    //
                    // extra_code
                    // Extra Space For Additional Code
                    // ram:08002640-ram:0800273f
                    //

                    gpioa_base
08002640 00 00 02 40     undefined4  40020000h

                    tim1_base
08002644 00 00 01 40     undefined4  40010000h
08002648 00              ??          00h
```

Fig.32

Save the changes and begin to write the patch. First, insert the label **test_pin** - this will be the point where our patch begins (**Fig.33**).

```
                    gpioa_base
08002640 00 00 02 40     undefined4 40020000h

                    timl_base
08002644 00 00 01 40     undefined4 40010000h

                    test_pin
08002648 00                ??          00h
08002649 00                ??          00h
0800264a 00                ??          00h
```

Fig.33

Next, we will write the code that will test pin **PA6** - this pin is free; therefore, we can use it. What we also need is to check if pin **PA6** is initialized as digital input (usually, after reset most GPIO pins of STM32Fxx MCUs are configured as digital inputs).

Checking the pin mode shows that **PA6** is already configured as input - this allows to simplify the code that will test the state of pin **PA6**.

Now we can write the patch. For typing an instruction, move a cursor to a target line, then right-click and select **Patch Instruction** (**Fig.34**) or simply press Ctrl+Shift+G.

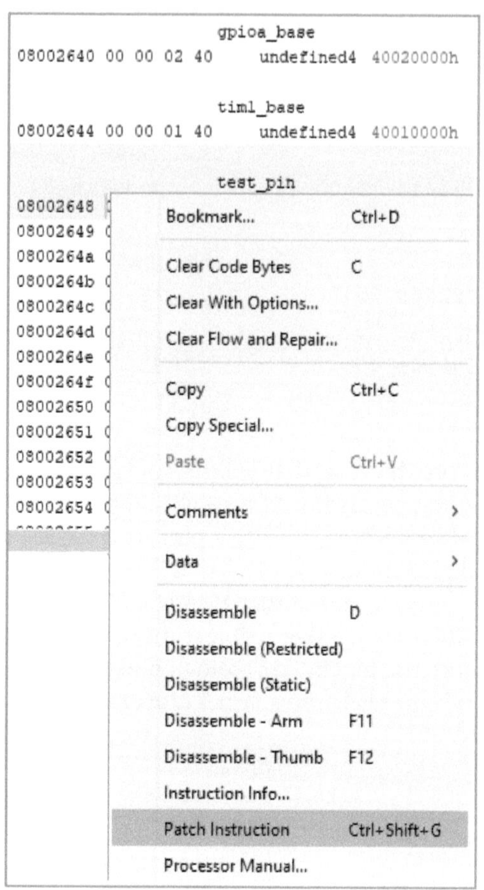

Fig.34

If this is the first instruction, GHIDRA issues the next warning (**Fig.35**).

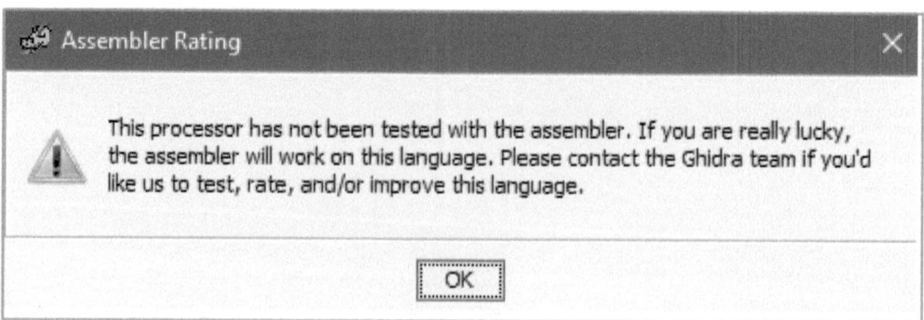

Fig.35

Simply press **OK** to continue. Then GHIDRA prepares the Assembler to process the instructions being patched (**Fig.36**). This may take a while.

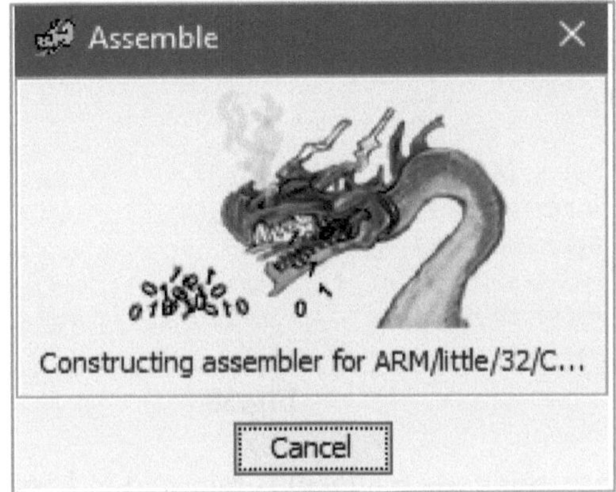

Fig.36

Let's type the code for testing pin **PA6**. GHIDRA provides the hints to autocomplete the instruction as is illustrated in **Fig.37**.

```
                          tim1_base
08002644 00 00 01 40         undefined4  40010000h

                          test_pin
08002648 00                  ldr.w    r0,[gpio
08002649 00                  ldr.w r0,[gpioa_base
0800264a 00
0800264b 00
0800264c 00
0800264d 00
0800264e 00
0800264f 00
08002650 00
08002651 00
08002652 00
08002653 00
08002654 00
```

Fig.37

When we are done, the code fragment testing digital input **PA6** will look like the following (**Fig.38**):

```
                     gpioa_base
08002640 00 00 02 40     undefined4 40020000h

                     tim1_base
08002644 00 00 01 40     undefined4 40010000h

                     test_pin
08002648 5f f8 0c 00     ldr.w       r0,[gpioa_base]
0800264c 00 f1 10 00     add.w       r0,r0,#0x10
08002650 01 68           ldr         r1,[r0,#0x0]
08002652 11 f0 40 0f     tst         r1,#0x40
08002656 f7 d0           beq         test_pin
08002658 00              ??          00h
```

Fig.38

For convenience, this code fragment is repeated in **Listing 5.**

Listing 5.

```
                // extra_code
                // Extra Space For Additional Code
                // ram:08002640-ram:0800273f
                //
                gpioa_base
08002640 00 00 02 40   undefined4 40020000h
                tim1_base
08002644 00 00 01 40   undefined4 40010000h
                test_pin
08002648        5f f8 0c 00     ldr.w   r0, [gpioa_base]    = 40020000h
0800264c        00 f1 10 00     add.w   r0, r0, #0x10
08002650        01 68           ldr     r1, [r0, #0x0]
08002652        11 f0 40 0f     tst     r1, #0x40
08002656        f7 d0           beq     test_pin
```

The first instruction in this sequence

```
ldr.w    r0, [gpioa_base]
```

loads the base address of port GPIOA in the core register **r0**. In order to read the state of input **PA6**, we then need to access register GPIO port input data register (GPIOA_IDR) with the offset +0x10 using the instruction

```
add.w   r0, r0, #0x10
```

After the instruction is executed, register **r0** contains the address of register GPIOA_IDR.
The next instruction loads the data from GPIOA_IDR into the core register **r1**:

```
ldr     r1, [r0, #0x0]
```

Pin **PA6** corresponds to bit 6 in register GPIOA_IDR, therefore we test this bit by instruction

```
tst     r1, #0x40
```

If this bit is cleared (=0), the branch instruction

```
beq     test_pin
```

passes control to the label **test_pin** and the loop repeats.
What happens if bit 6 is set (=1) is shown in the following code fragment (rectangle in **Fig.39**).

```
                    gpioa_base
08002640 00 00 02 40     undefined4  40020000h

                    tim1_base
08002644 00 00 01 40     undefined4  40010000h

                    test_pin
08002648 5f f8 0c 00     ldr.w       r0,[gpioa_base]
0800264c 00 f1 10 00     add.w       r0,r0,#0x10
08002650 01 68           ldr         r1,[r0,#0x0]
08002652 11 f0 40 0f     tst         r1,#0x40
08002656 f7 d0           beq         test_pin
08002658 5f f8 18 00     ldr.w       r0,[tim1_base]
0800265c 00 f1 20 00     add.w       r0,r0,#0x20
08002660 01 68           ldr         r1,[r0,#0x0]
08002662 6f f3 00 01     bfc         r1,#0x0,#0x1
08002666 01 60           str         r1,[r0,#0x0]
08002668 00              ??          00h
```

Fig.39

For convenience, the selected code fragment is repeated in **Listing 6.**

Listing 6.

```
08002658    5f f8 18 00    ldr.w    r0, [tim1_base]   = 40010000h
0800265c    00 f1 20 00    add.w    r0, r0, #0x20
08002660    01 68          ldr      r1, [r0, #0x0]
08002662    6f f3 00 01    bfc      r1, #0x0, #0x1
08002666    01 60          str      r1, [r0, #0x0]
```

The above code fragment will be executed when bit 6 of register GPIOA_IDR (pin **PA6**) is set (=1). This code stops generating the PWM signal on Channel 1 output of Timer 1 by clearing bit 0 (CC1**E**) in the TIM1 capture/compare enable register (TIM1_CCER).
This register has the address offset = 0x20, therefore the sequence

```
ldr.w    r0, [tim1_base]
add.w    r0, r0, #0x20
```

loads the address of TIM1_CCER into the core register **r0**.
Then the instruction

```
ldr     r1, [r0, #0x0]
```

loads the data held in TIM1_CCER into register **r1**. To stop the Channel 1 output, we clear bit 0 by the following instruction:

```
bfc     r1, #0x0, #0x1
```

The last instruction in this sequence

```
str     r1, [r0, #0x0]
```

writes the updated value of **r1** into register TIM1_CCER thus disabling the PWM signal on pin **PE9**.
After the **str** instruction we insert the branch instruction (**Fig.40**) that puts the application into the infinite loop (label **loop_1**).

```
                        loop_1
08002668 fe e7               b            loop_1
0800266a 00                  ??           00h
```

Fig.40

The whole patch is shown in **Listing 7**.

Listing 7.

```
                // extra_code
                // Extra Space For Additional Code
                // ram:08002640-ram:0800273f
                //
                gpioa_base
08002640    00 00 02 40    undefined4   40020000h
                tim1_base
08002644    00 00 01 40    undefined4   40010000h
                test_pin
08002648        5f f8 0c 00       ldr.w     r0, [gpioa_base]     = 40020000h
```

```
0800264c        00 f1 10 00     add.w  r0, r0, #0x10
08002650        01 68           ldr    r1, [r0, #0x0]
08002652        11 f0 40 0f     tst    r1, #0x40
08002656        f7 d0           beq    test_pin
08002658        5f f8 18 00     ldr.w  r0, [tim1_base]   = 40010000h
0800265c        00 f1 20 00     add.w  r0, r0, #0x20
08002660        01 68           ldr    r1, [r0, #0x0]
08002662        6f f3 00 01     bfc    r1, #0x0, #0x1
08002666        01 60           str    r1, [r0, #0x0]
                loop_1
08002668        fe e7           b      loop_1
0800266a        00              ??     00h
```

Now we need to rewrite a branch instruction in the **main()** function (**Listing 8**) in order pass control to label **test_pin**.

Listing 8.

```
                LAB_08000534
08000534        fe e7           b      LAB_08000534
08000536        00              ??     00h
08000537        00              ??     00h
```

We will replace instruction

```
08000534        fe e7           b      LAB_08000534
```

by

```
08000534        02 f0 88 b8     b.w    test_pin
```

as is shown below (arrow in **Fig.41**).

```
08000524 00 f0 d7 fa     bl       FUN_08000ad6
08000528 00 f0 06 f8     bl       FUN_08000538
0800052c 00 f0 08 f9     bl       FUN_08000740
08000530 00 f0 70 f8     bl       FUN_08000614
08000534 02 f0 88 b8     b.w      test_pin  <----
```

Fig.41

Now the 4-byte instruction

b.w   test_pin

branches to label **test_pin**.
The high-level representation of the modified code can be viewed in the **Decompile** window (**Fig.42**).

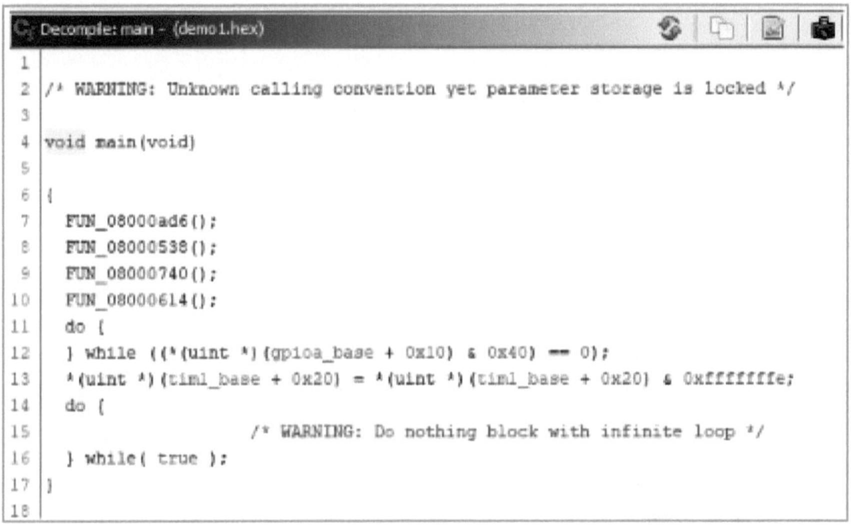

```
Decompile: main - (demo1.hex)

/* WARNING: Unknown calling convention yet parameter storage is locked */

void main(void)

{
  FUN_08000ad6();
  FUN_08000538();
  FUN_08000740();
  FUN_08000614();
  do {
  } while ((*(uint *)(gpioa_base + 0x10) & 0x40) == 0);
  *(uint *)(tim1_base + 0x20) = *(uint *)(tim1_base + 0x20) & 0xfffffffe;
  do {
                    /* WARNING: Do nothing block with infinite loop */
  } while( true );
}
```

Fig.42

The block diagram in **Fig.43** summarizes what we did.

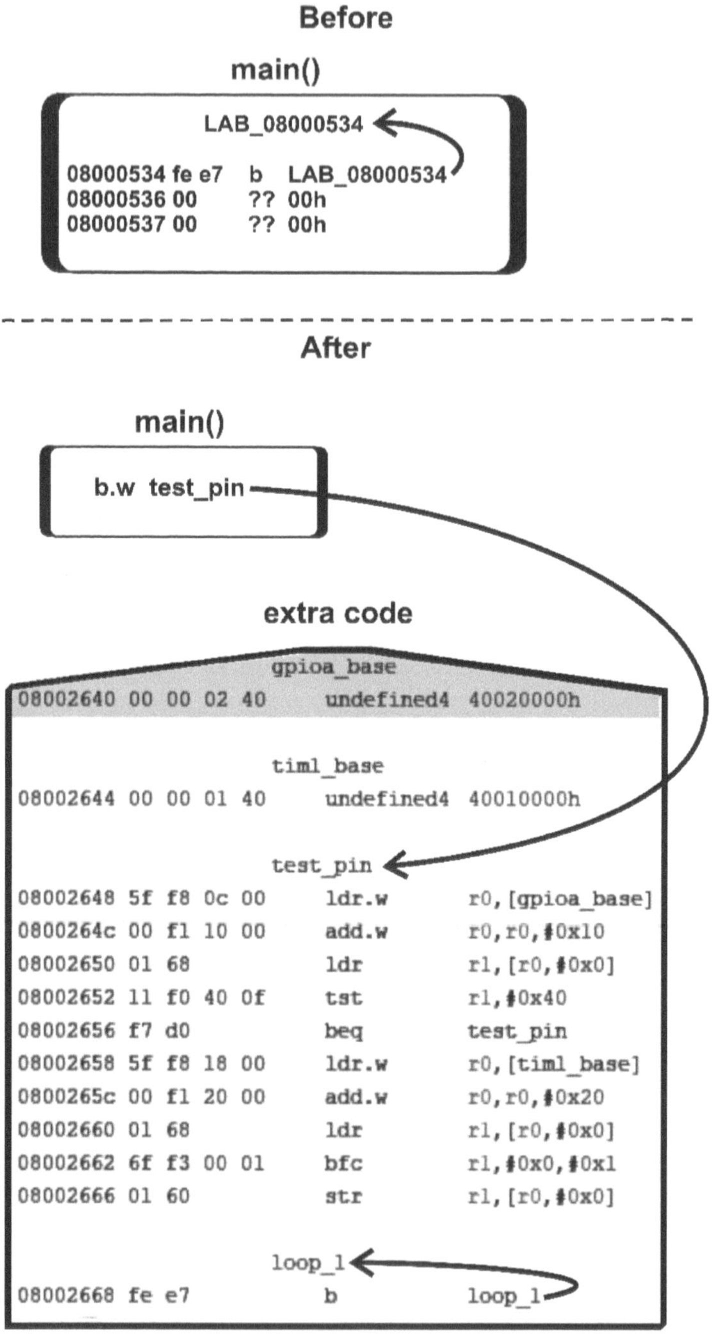

Before

main()

```
            LAB_08000534
08000534 fe e7    b   LAB_08000534
08000536 00       ??  00h
08000537 00       ??  00h
```

After

main()

```
b.w  test_pin
```

extra code

```
                        gpioa_base
08002640 00 00 02 40       undefined4  40020000h

                        tim1_base
08002644 00 00 01 40       undefined4  40010000h

                        test_pin
08002648 5f f8 0c 00       ldr.w       r0,[gpioa_base]
0800264c 00 f1 10 00       add.w       r0,r0,#0x10
08002650 01 68             ldr         r1,[r0,#0x0]
08002652 11 f0 40 0f       tst         r1,#0x40
08002656 f7 d0             beq         test_pin
08002658 5f f8 18 00       ldr.w       r0,[tim1_base]
0800265c 00 f1 20 00       add.w       r0,r0,#0x20
08002660 01 68             ldr         r1,[r0,#0x0]
08002662 6f f3 00 01       bfc         r1,#0x0,#0x1
08002666 01 60             str         r1,[r0,#0x0]

                        loop_1
08002668 fe e7             b           loop_1
```

Fig.43

Next, we need to export the modified binary into a HEX file and then download this file into the MCU flash memory.
To export the binary, select **File→Export Program…** option in **CodeBrowser** (**Fig.44**).

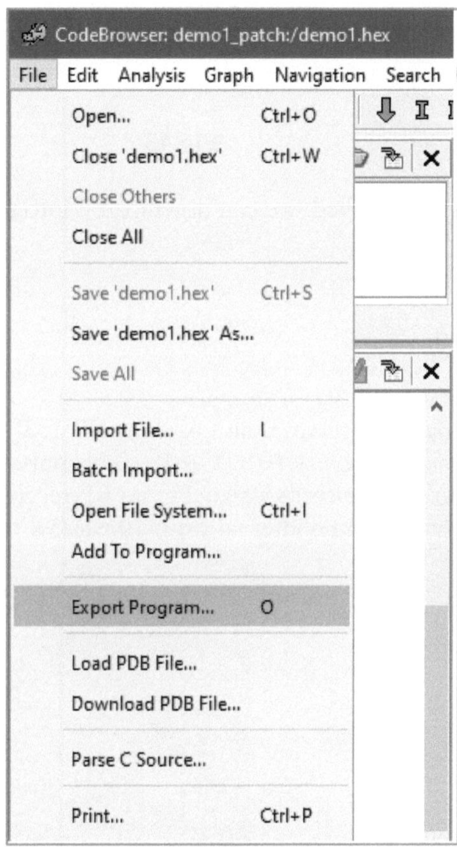

Fig.44

In the opened window (**Fig.45**), select the **Intel HEX** format and choose the full path to this file.

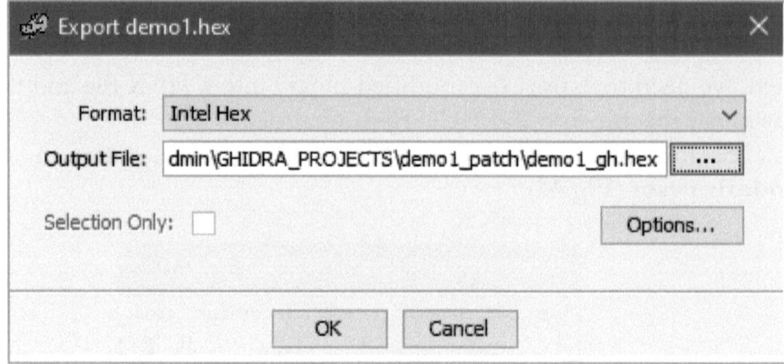

Fig.45

Once the HEX file is saved, we can download it into the MCU flash memory.

Example 2

An existing embedded system built upon the STM32F030 MCU produces a short pulse on pin **PA1** every 10 s (**Fig.46**). This pulse activates the RF transmitter that then transmits a signal to an RF receiver on a host computer. We need to reduce the time interval from 10 s to 5 s.

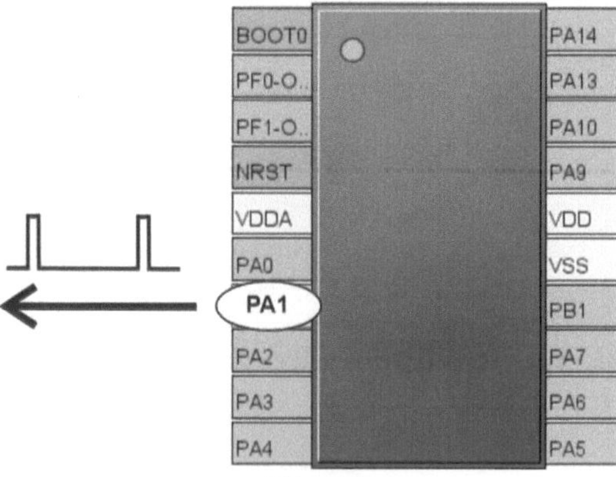

Fig.46

Since the application uses pin **PA1** of port GPIOA, we will probably deal either with GPIO_ODR or GPIO_BSRR memory-mapped register of STM32F030.
It seems reasonable to assume that the periodical signal on pin **PA1** may be synchronized by some clocking systems. The common method to implement such synchronization is to apply a timer. It is possible, however, to use some delays within a **while()/for()** loop to toggle a pin, but in practice such approach is rarely used.

Let's begin to analyze an existing binary (HEX file).

Analyzing a binary

As in the previous example, to analyze the HEX file (named **demo2.hex**) we first need to create the GHIDRA project and import this file into the project (**Fig.47**).

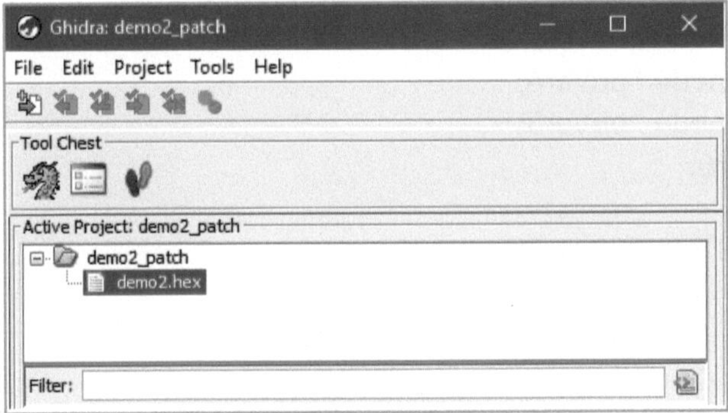

Fig.47

Also, we select the ARM:v8T:32:LE:default assembler language (**Fig.48**).

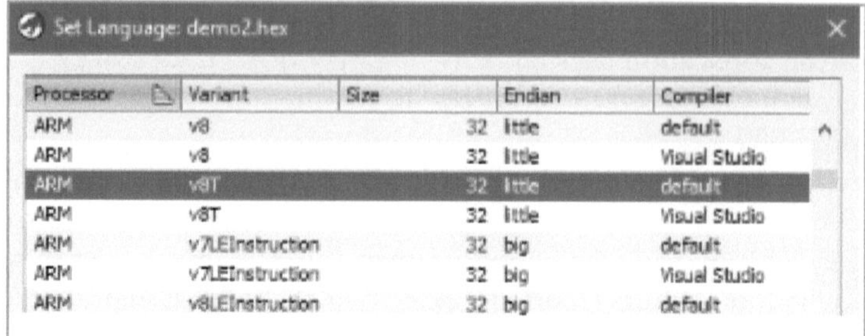

Fig.48

Then we find the **entry()** function whose code taken from the **Decompile** window. is shown in **Listing 9**.

Listing 9.

```
void entry(void)
{
  int iVar1;
  uint uVar2;
  undefined *puVar3;
  undefined4 *puVar4;
  undefined4 *puVar5;
  int iVar6;

  puVar3 = PTR_DAT_08000444;
  uVar2 = DAT_08000440;
  iVar1 = DAT_0800043c;
  iVar6 = 0;
  while (puVar4 = DAT_0800044c, puVar5 = DAT_08000448, (uint)(iVar1 +
iVar6) < uVar2) {
    *(undefined4 *)(iVar1 + iVar6) = *(undefined4 *)(puVar3 + iVar6);
    iVar6 = iVar6 + 4;
  }
  while (puVar5 < puVar4) {
    *puVar5 = 0;
    puVar5 = puVar5 + 1;
  }
  FUN_080003f4();
```

```
  FUN_08000f20();
  FUN_08000220();
  do {
              /* WARNING: Do nothing block with infinite loop */
  } while( true );
}
```

From this listing, it seems reasonable to assume that the best candidate for the **main()** function is **FUN_08000220()**. Double-clicking on this function gives us the **Decompile** code (**Listing 10**).

Listing 10.

```
void FUN_08000220(void)
{
  FUN_08000454();
  FUN_08000288();
  *(uint *)(DAT_08000284 + 0x14) = *(uint *)(DAT_08000284 + 0x14) |
                                                  0x20000;
  do {
              /* WARNING: Do nothing block with infinite loop */
  } while( true );
}
```

While looking at the disassembly of **FUN_08000220**, we may notice the fragment (**Listing 11**) corresponding to the statement.

```
*(uint *)(DAT_080002a0 + 0x14) = *(uint *)(DAT_080002a0 + 0x14) |
                                                  0x20000;
```

from the **Decompile** window. For convenience, we break the whole disassembly down into a few fragments as is shown in **Listing 11**.

Listing 11.

Fragment 1

```
0800022c      15 4b    ldr      r3, [DAT_08000284]      = 40021000h
```

```
0800022e	5a 69	ldr	r2, [r3, #offset DAT_40021014]
08000230	14 4b	ldr	r3, [DAT_08000284]		= 40021000h
08000232	80 21	mov	r1, #0x80
08000234	89 02	lsl	r1, r1, #0xa
08000236	0a 43	orr	r2, r1
08000238	5a 61	str	r2, [r3, #offset DAT_40021014]
```

Fragment 2

```
0800023a	90 23	mov	r3, #0x90
0800023c	db 05	lsl	r3, r3, #0x17
0800023e	1a 68	ldr	r2, [r3, #0x0] =>DAT_48000000
08000240	90 23	mov	r3, #0x90
08000242	db 05	lsl	r3, r3, #0x17
08000244	04 21	mov	r1, #0x4
08000246	0a 43	orr	r2, r1
08000248	1a 60	str	r2, [r3, #0x0] =>DAT_48000000
```

Fragment 3

```
0800024a	90 23	mov	r3, #0x90
0800024c	db 05	lsl	r3, r3, #0x17
0800024e	5a 68	ldr	r2, [r3, #offset DAT_48000004]
08000250	90 23	mov	r3, #0x90
08000252	db 05	lsl	r3, r3, #0x17
08000254	02 21	mov	r1, #0x2
08000256	8a 43	bic	r2, r1
08000258	5a 60	str	r2, [r3, #offset DAT_48000004]
```

Fragment 4

```
0800025a	90 23	mov	r3, #0x90
0800025c	db 05	lsl	r3, r3, #0x17
0800025e	da 68	ldr	r2, [r3, #offset DAT_4800000c]
08000260	90 23	mov	r3, #0x90
08000262	db 05	lsl	r3, r3, #0x17
08000264	0c 21	mov	r1, #0xc
```

```
08000266        8a 43   bic     r2, r1
08000268        da 60   str     r2, [r3, #offset DAT_4800000c]
```

Fragment 5

```
0800026a        90 23   mov     r3, #0x90
0800026c        db 05   lsl     r3, r3, #0x17
0800026e        9a 68   ldr     r2, [r3, #offset DAT_48000008]
08000270        90 23   mov     r3, #0x90
08000272        db 05   lsl     r3, r3, #0x17
08000274        04 21   mov     r1, #0x4
08000276        0a 43   orr     r2, r1
08000278        9a 60   str     r2, [r3, #offset DAT_48000008]
```

Fragment 6

```
0800027a        90 23   mov     r3, #0x90
0800027c        db 05   lsl     r3, r3, #0x17
0800027e        02 22   mov     r2, #0x2
08000280        9a 62   str     r2, [r3, #offset DAT_48000028]
```

In the above disassembly, each fragment begins with the **ldr** instruction and ends up with the **str** instruction. After analyzing, it turns out that the code in **Fragment 1** enables clocking of port GPIOA by writing 1 into bit 17 of the AHB peripheral clock enable register (RCC_AHBENR) whose address is 0x40021014.

In **Fragment 1**, the sequence

```
0800022c        15 4b   ldr     r3, [DAT_08000284]          = 40021000h
0800022e        5a 69   ldr     r2, [r3, #offset DAT_40021014]
```

loads the value stored in RCC_AHBENR into the core register **r2** for further processing.

The sequence

```
08000232        80 21   mov     r1, #0x80
08000234        89 02   lsl     r1, r1, #0xa
```

seems a bit odd, but it simply writes 0x1 into bit 17 in the core register **r1**. Then the instruction

```
08000236        0a 43    orr     r2, r1
```

writes 0x1 into bit 17 of register **r2**. Finally, the instruction

```
08000238        5a 61    str     r2, [r3, #offset DAT_40021014]
```

write the updated value in **r2** into register RCC_AHBENR - this enables the clock of port GPIOA.
Traversing the rest of the disassembly in **Listing 11** proves that all operations use address 0x48000000 that is a base address of port GPIOA. Therefore, it seems reasonable to assume that the instructions in **Fragments 2** - **6** perform the initialization of port GPIOA.
The code in **Fragment 2** begins with the instructions

```
0800023a        90 23    mov     r3, #0x90
0800023c        db 05    lsl     r3, r3, #0x17
```

that load the base address of port GPIOA (=0x48000000) into the core register **r3** (0x90 << 0x17 = 0x48000000).
Then the instruction

```
0800023e        1a 68    ldr     r2, [r3, #0x0] =>DAT_48000000
```

loads the value in 0x48000000 into **r2** for further processing.
The value in register **r2** is then modified by the sequence

```
08000244        04 21    mov     r1, #0x4
08000246        0a 43    orr     r2, r1
```

Finally, the value held in **r2** is written back into the address 0x48000000 by the instruction

```
08000248        1a 60    str     r2, [r3, #0x0]=>DAT_48000000
```

Since the base address 0x48000000 is also the address of the GPIO port mode register (GPIOA_MODER), then writing the value 0x4 into this register configures bit 1 of GPIOA (pin **PA1**) as general-purpose output.

Thus, the code in **Fragment 2** configures pin **PA1** as output.
Further analyzing shows that **Fragments 3** - **5** provide additional settings for pin **PA1**.
The code in **Fragment 6** writes the value 0x0 into pin **PA1** using the GPIO port bit reset register (GPIOx_BRR) whose address is 0x48000000+0x28 = 0x48000028.
From the disassembly shown in **Listing 11**, we can conclude that the code in the **main()** function implements initialization for pin **PA1**. It also becomes clear that toggling **PA1** is performed elsewhere, therefore we need to analyze other fragments of disassembly in order to find some references to this pin and/or port GPIOA.
To begin search, select **Search→ Program Text...** (**Fig.49**).

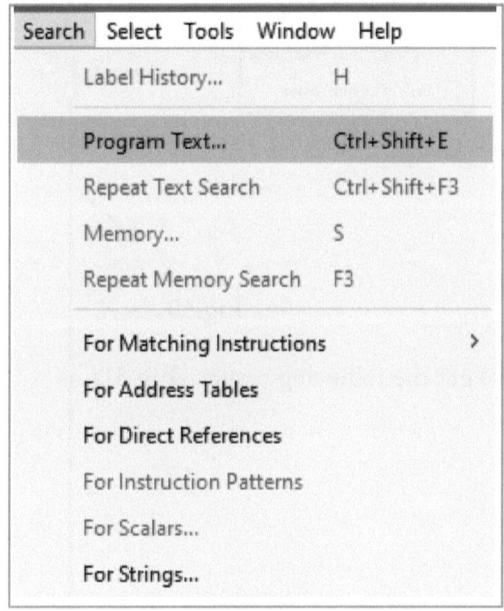

Fig.49

In the next window, select the fields in rectangle (**Fig.50**) and type **DAT_4800** in field **Search for:**, then click **Search All**.

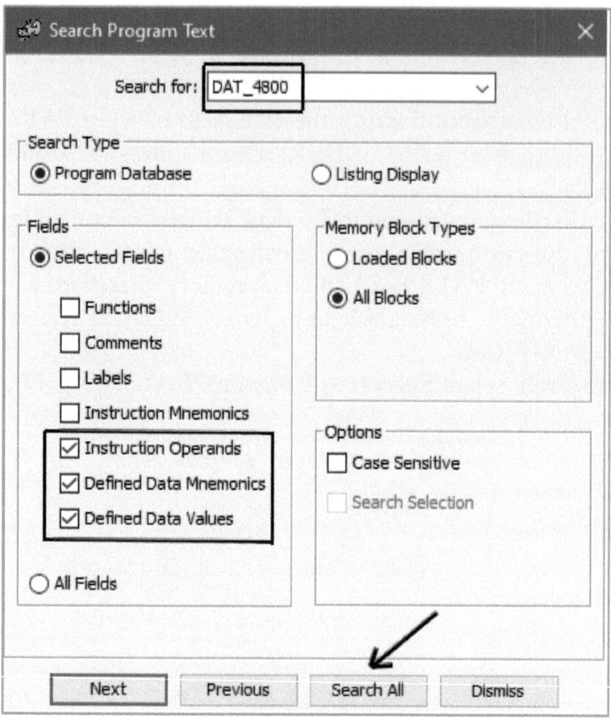

Fig.50

In our case, we get the following results (**Fig.51)**.

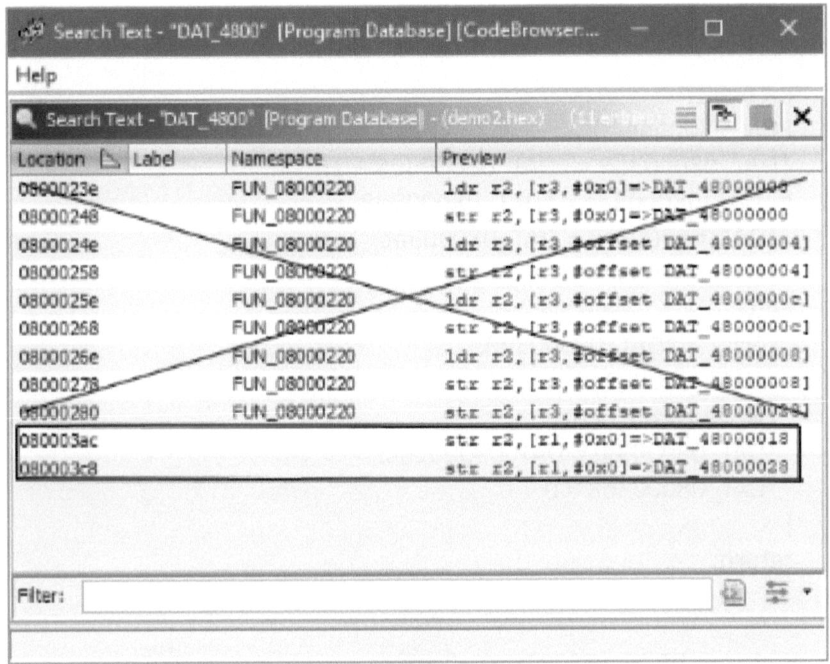

Fig.51

We will not analyze the records with **FUN_08000220** (a crossed-out area), but the following 2 addresses

080003ac
080003c8

must be checked.
Double-clicking on **080003ac** brings us to the following instruction

```
080003ac        0a 60    str       r2, [r1, #0x0] =>DAT_48000018
```

The further analysis shows that instruction belongs to function **FUN_0800038c()** whose source code produced by GHIDRA Decompiler is shown in **Listing 12.**

Listing 12.

```
void FUN_0800038c(void)
```

```
{
 int iVar1;
 FUN_080004e4();
 *DAT_080003d8 = *DAT_080003d8 + 1;
 if (DAT_080003dc < *DAT_080003d8) {
  *DAT_080003e8 = DAT_080003ec;
  *DAT_080003e0 = DAT_080003e4;
  do {
   iVar1 = *DAT_080003e0;
   *DAT_080003e0 = iVar1 + -1;
  } while (iVar1 != 0);
  *DAT_080003f0 = DAT_080003ec;
  *DAT_080003d8 = 0;
 }
 return;
}
```

Analyzing **FUN_0800038c()** allows to assume that its code can process some event / exception. This function is not called from any other function, because there are no references to **FUN_0800038c() in** the **Symbol Table** window (**Fig.52**). It is reasonable to assume that function **FUN_0800038c()** is nothing else but a **SysTick Event Handler** that is called every 1 mS (by default).

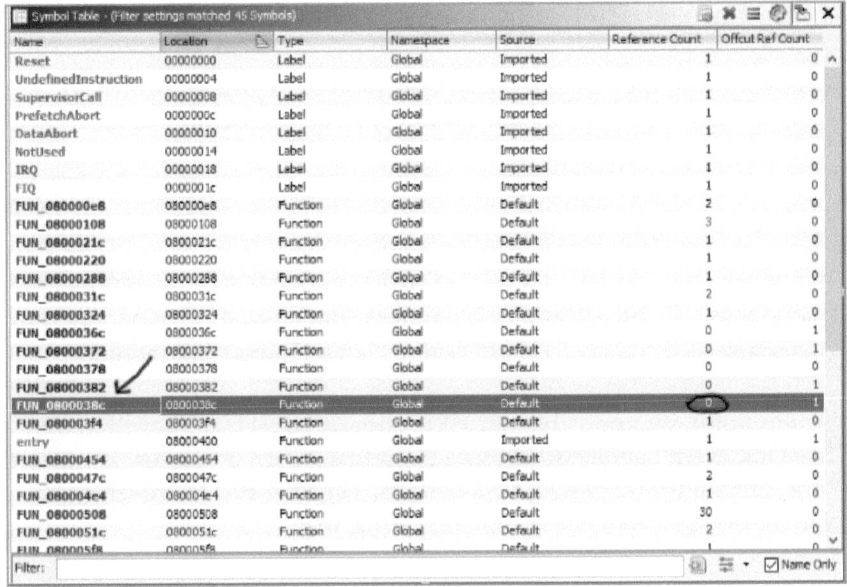
Symbol Table - (Filter settings matched 45 Symbols)

Name	Location	Type	Namespace	Source	Reference Count	Offcut Ref Count
Reset	00000000	Label	Global	Imported	1	0
UndefinedInstruction	00000004	Label	Global	Imported	1	0
SupervisorCall	00000008	Label	Global	Imported	1	0
PrefetchAbort	0000000c	Label	Global	Imported	1	0
DataAbort	00000010	Label	Global	Imported	1	0
NotUsed	00000014	Label	Global	Imported	1	0
IRQ	00000018	Label	Global	Imported	1	0
FIQ	0000001c	Label	Global	Imported	1	0
FUN_080000e8	080000e8	Function	Global	Default	2	0
FUN_08000108	08000108	Function	Global	Default	3	0
FUN_0800021c	0800021c	Function	Global	Default	1	0
FUN_08000220	08000220	Function	Global	Default	1	0
FUN_08000288	08000288	Function	Global	Default	1	0
FUN_0800031c	0800031c	Function	Global	Default	2	0
FUN_08000324	08000324	Function	Global	Default	1	0
FUN_0800036c	0800036c	Function	Global	Default	0	1
FUN_08000372	08000372	Function	Global	Default	0	1
FUN_08000378	08000378	Function	Global	Default	0	0
FUN_08000382	08000382	Function	Global	Default	0	1
FUN_0800038c	0800038c	Function	Global	Default	0	1
FUN_080003f4	080003f4	Function	Global	Default	1	0
entry	08000400	Function	Global	Imported	1	1
FUN_08000454	08000454	Function	Global	Default	1	0
FUN_0800047c	0800047c	Function	Global	Default	2	0
FUN_080004e4	080004e4	Function	Global	Default	1	0
FUN_08000508	08000508	Function	Global	Default	30	0
FUN_0800051c	0800051c	Function	Global	Default	2	0
FUN_080005f8	080005f8	Function	Global	Default	1	0

Filter: Name Only

Fig.52

First what we will need to determine is how the code in function **FUN_0800038c()** affects port GPIOA. Traversing the code gives us a few statements that access GPIOA.
The statement

```
*DAT_080003e8 = DAT_080003ec;
```

is broken down into the following sequence of MCU instructions (**Listing 13**).

Listing 13.

```
080003a8    0f 49   ldr    r1, [DAT_080003e8]       = 48000018h
080003aa    10 4a   ldr    r2, [DAT_080003ec]       = 00000002h
080003ac    0a 60   str    r2, [r1, #0x0]=>DAT_48000018
```

This sequence writes 0x1 into bit 1 of the GPIO port bit set/reset register (GPIOA_BSRR, 0x48000018) thus bringing pin **PA1** HIGH.
One more statement

```
*DAT_080003f0 = DAT_080003ec;
```

writes 0x1 into bit 1 of the GPIO port bit reset register (GPIOA_BRR, 0x48000028) thus bringing pin **PA1** LOW. The disassembly of this statement is shown in **Listing 14**.

Listing 14.

```
080003c4    0a 49   ldr   r1, [DAT_080003f0]      = 48000028h
080003c6    09 4a   ldr   r2, [DAT_080003ec]      = 00000002h
080003c8    0a 60   str   r2, [r1, #0x0] =>DAT_48000028
```

At this point, we know that pin **PA1** is driven HIGH/LOW within the **SysTick** event handler. One more thing that we need to know is where the time interval for toggling **PA1** is defined. Toggling **PA1** is implemented within the **if()** statement shown in **Listing 15**.

Listing 15.

```
if (DAT_080003dc < *DAT_080003d8)
{
  .......
}
```

The **if()** disassembly is shown in **Listing 16**.

Listing 16.

```
080003a0    1b 68   ldr   r3, [r3, #0x0] =>DAT_20000028
080003a2    0e 4a   ldr   r2, [DAT_080003dc]   = 00002710h
080003a4    93 42   cmp   r3, r2
080003a6    13 d9   bls   LAB_080003d0
```

In the above code, the value held at address 0x20000028 is moved into register **r3**, and the constant 0x2710 (=10000) is moved into register **r2**. The **cmp** instruction compares values in **r3** and **r2**. If **r3** < **r2**, the function returns by branching to label **LAB_080003d0** without affecting pin **PA1**. If **r3** ≥ **r2**, the short pulse is produced on pin **PA1**.

Thus, when the value at the address 0x20000028 reaches 10000, the code within the **if()** statement toggles pin **PA1**.
Before the **if()** statement begins to execute, the value at address 0x20000028 is incremented by 1. That is done by the following statement

```
*DAT_080003d8 = *DAT_080003d8 + 1;
```

The disassembly of this statement is shown in **Listing 17**.

Listing 17.

```
08000394    10 4b   ldr    r3, [DAT_080003d8]      = 20000028h
08000396    1b 68   ldr    r3, [r3, #0x0] =>DAT_20000028
08000398    5a 1c   add    r2, r3, #0x1
0800039a    0f 4b   ldr    r3, [DAT_080003d8]      = 20000028h
0800039c    1a 60   str    r2, [r3, #0x0] =>DAT_20000028
```

In this code fragment, the address 0x20000028 is loaded into register **r3**, then the value at this address is stored in **r3**.
The **add** instruction increments the value in register **r3** by 1 and stores the result in register **r2**. Finally, the updated value (register **r2**) is written back to the address 0x20000028.

Patching a HEX file

At this point we have enough information to patch the code. To reduce the interval of 10 s between toggling **PA1** to 5 s, we need to change the value at location **DAT_080003dc**. Instead of 0x2710 (=10000), we need to write 0x1388 (=5000) - this corresponds to the 5 s interval.
To modify the value, we place the cursor at this location (**Fig.53**), then open the **Display Bytes** window (**Fig.54**) and edit the required fields. The **DAT_080003dc** location will then contain the value 0x1388 (**Fig.55**).

Fig.53

Fig.54

Fig.55

Save the changes and export the whole memory block into the HEX file. The file is then ready to be downloaded into the flash memory of MCU.

Example 3

The embedded system built upon an ATSAMD21G18A (Cortex-M0+) microcontroller generates a short pulse on pin **PA20** to drive the power circuit ON after 3000 mS after the system has been started as is illustrated in **Fig.56**.

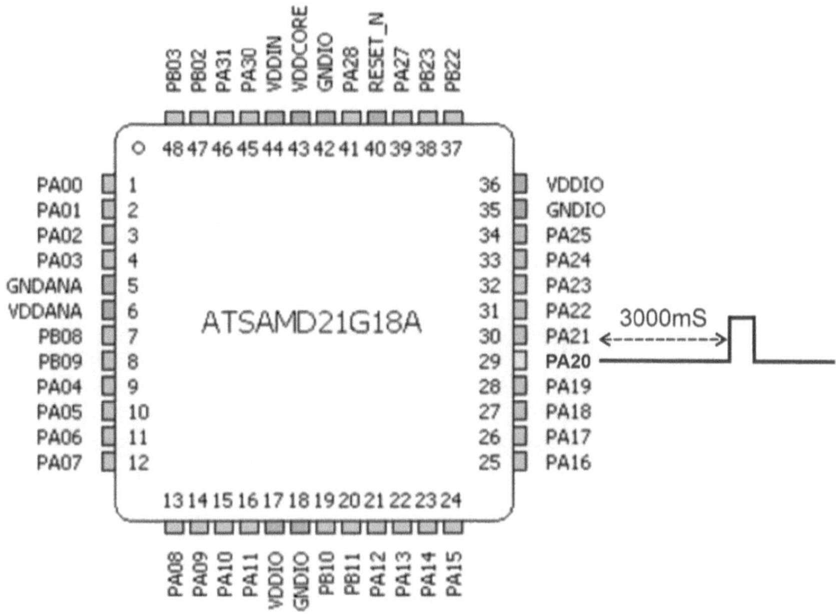

Fig.56

We need to increase the start delay from 3000 mS to at least 7200 mS (**Fig.57**).

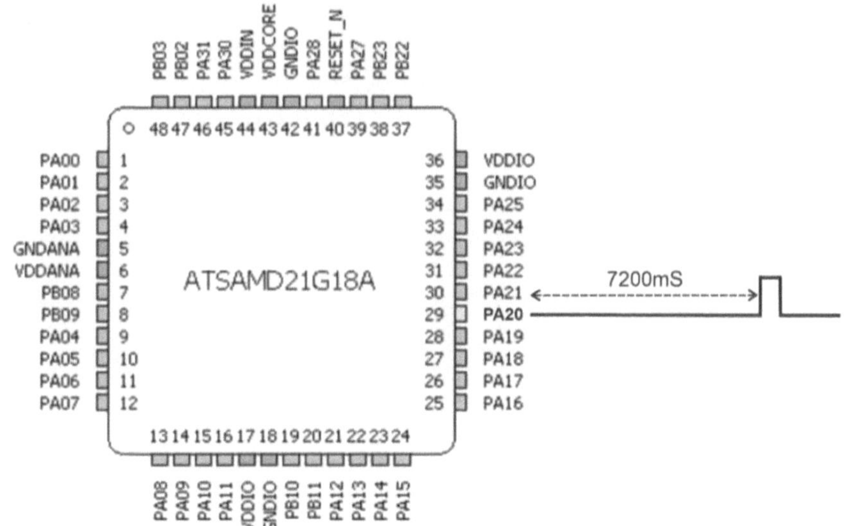

Fig.57

Analyzing a binary

As in the previous examples, we create a new project in GHIDRA (named **demo3_patch**) and add the HEX file (named **demo3.hex**) to it. For this project, we select the ARM:v8T:32:LE language (**Fig.58**).

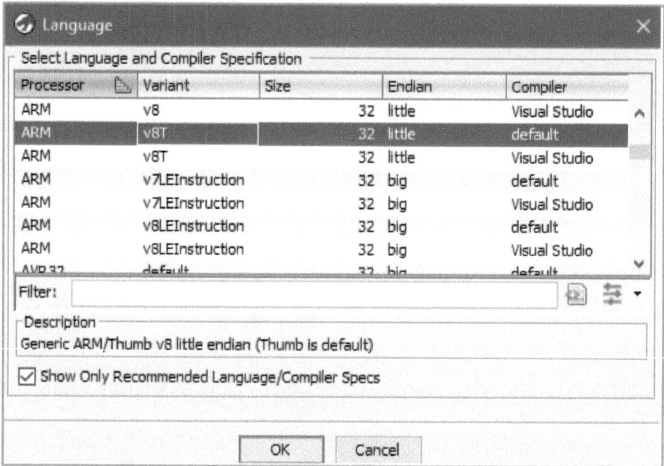

Fig.58

Before analyzing the binary in the **CodeBrowser**, we enable the **ARM Aggressive Instruction Finder (Prototype)** option (**Fig.59**) in order to improve the quality of the disassembly being generated.

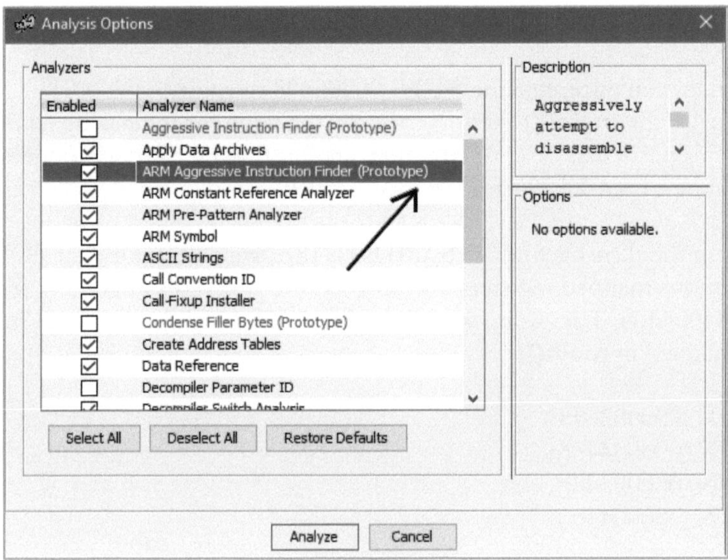

Fig.59

After the GHIDRA completes the analysis of the binary, we save data and begin to analyze the code in detail.

First, we determine where the **main()** code begins by traversing the **Symbol Tree** window. It seems reasonable to assume that the best candidate for **main()** is function **FUN_00000408** (**Listing 18**).

Listing 18.

```
void FUN_00000408(void)
{
  FUN_000003e0(0);
  FUN_00000448();
  *(uint *)(DAT_00000428 + 0x10) = *(uint *)(DAT_00000428 + 0x10) &
            DAT_0000042c;
  FUN_00000348();
  FUN_00000430();
  do {
            /* WARNING: Do nothing block with infinite loop */
  } while( true );
```

}

For convenience, rename **FUN_00000408** to **main**.
Usually, the **main**() function contains the code for initializing all peripherals. In this particular case, we are interested in finding the code fragments relating to pin **PA20** of a microcontroller.

From the datasheet on ATSAMD21G18A, we determine that PORTA memory-mapped registers are assigned the addresses beginning from 0x41004400. Therefore, we will search for these addresses in all functions contained in **main()**:

```
FUN_000003e0(0);
FUN_00000448();
FUN_00000348();
FUN_00000430();
```

Particularly, the disassembly of function **FUN_00000448()** gives us the following (**Listing 19**):

Listing 19.

```
**************************************************
*                    FUNCTION                    *
**************************************************
undefined FUN_00000448()
FUN_00000448                XREF[2]:  FUN_000003e0:000003e8(c),
                                      main:00000410(c)

00000448    80 22   mov   r2, #0x80
0000044a    52 03   lsl   r2, r2, #0xd
0000044c    01 4b   ldr   r3, [DAT_00000454]      = 41004400h
0000044e    1a 60   str   r2, [r3, #0x0] =>DAT_41004400
00000450    70 47   bx    lr
```

The above code simply configures pin **PA20** of PORTA as output by writing 0x1 into bit 20 of port DIR that has the offset +0x0 from the base address 0x41004400.

Let's look at the following sequence that goes after the **FUN_00000448()** call (**Listing 20**).

Listing 20.

```
00000414    04 4a   ldr    r2, [DAT_00000428]        = 41004400h
00000416    13 69   ldr    r3, [r2, #offset DAT_41004410]
00000418    04 49   ldr    r1, [DAT_0000042c]        = FFEFFFFFh
0000041a    0b 40   and    r3, r1
0000041c    13 61   str    r3, [r2, #offset DAT_41004410]
```

This sequence simply clears bit 20 in register OUT of PORTA thus bringing pin **PA20** LOW.

At this point, we exactly know how pin **PA20** is initialized, but we don't know what PORTA register is used to write data to this pin. Therefore, we will search for the program text **DAT_410044**, **41004410h** and **41004418h.** The values **41004410h** and **41004418h** are associated with the registers OUT and OUTSET of PORTA, respectively. Each of these registers may be used in write operations. Unluckily, no function listed in the **Symbol Tree** window contains these data.
This situation often means that the data/code of interest may be located elsewhere, so we should traverse overall code once more and seek where pin **PA20** is toggled.
The disassembly contains a few unidentified memory blocks containing some byte sequences. One of these blocks is shown in **Listing 21**.

Listing 21.

```
DAT_000000bc                  XREF[2]:   FUN_00000300:00000326(R),
                                         FUN_00000300:00000330(R)
000000bc    e1 02 00 00    undefined4 000002E1h    ? -> 000002e1
000000c0    f8       ??    F8h
000000c1    b5       ??    B5h
000000c2    c0       ??    C0h
000000c3    46       ??    46h      F
000000c4    f8       ??    F8h
000000c5    bc       ??    BCh
000000c6    08       ??    08h
```

000000c7	bc	??	BCh		
000000c8	9e	??	9Eh		
000000c9	46	??	46h	F	
000000ca	70	??	70h	p	
000000cb	47	??	47h	G	
000000cc	b9	??	B9h		? -> 000002b9
000000cd	02	??	02h		
000000ce	00	??	00h		
000000cf	00	??	00h		

Frequently, such unidentified memory blocks contain some system code and/or exception handlers. Probably, the code that we seek is located in one of these blocks.

Let's disassemble the memory block shown in **Listing 21** manually. To do that, place the cursor at the first address that may contain the code, then right-click and select the desired option (in our case, **Disassemble** - **Thumb** in **Fig.60**).

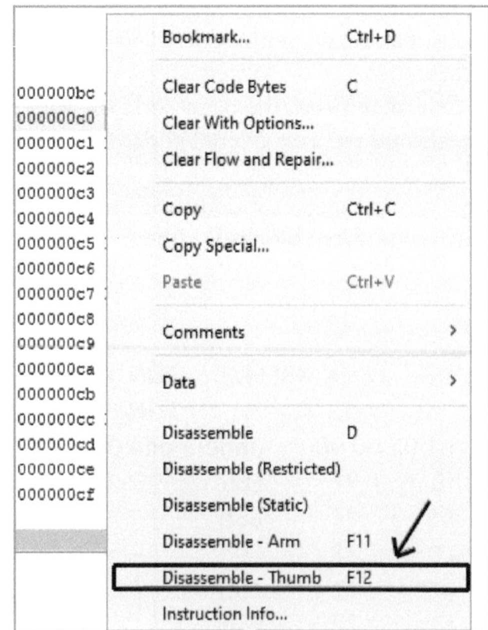

Fig.60

When we are done, the disassembly of the above memory block looks like the following (**Listing 22**):

Listing 22.

```
000000c0    f8 b5   push    { r3, r4, r5, r6, r7, lr }
000000c2    c0 46   mov     r8,r8
000000c4    f8 bc   pop     { r3, r4, r5, r6, r7 }
000000c6    08 bc   pop     { r3 }
000000c8    9e 46   mov     lr,r3
000000ca    70 47   bx      lr
000000cc    b9      ??      B9h     ? -> 000002b9
000000cd    02      ??      02h
000000ce    00      ??      00h
000000cf    00      ??      00h
```

It is seen that the above disassembly gives us the code of a function that does nothing. The sequence in **Listing 22** contains only the prolog and epilog code of the function, therefore we skip this block continue to search for the data relating to PORTA.

After disassembling a few unidentified memory blocks, we finally get the interesting disassembly beginning at address 00000204 (**Listing 23**).

Listing 23.

```
00000204    0f 4b   ldr     r3, [DAT_00000244]      = 42003000h
00000206    9a 7b   ldrb    r2, [r3, #offset DAT_4200300e]
00000208    3b 22   mov     r2, #0x3b
0000020a    9a 73   strb    r2, [r3, #offset DAT_4200300e]
0000020c    0e 4a   ldr     r2, [DAT_00000248]      = 20000024h
0000020e    13 68   ldr     r3, [r2, #0x0] =>DAT_20000024
00000210    59 1c   add     r1, r3, #0x1
00000212    11 60   str     r1, [r2, #0x0] =>DAT_20000024
00000214    0d 4a   ldr     r2, [DAT_0000024c]      = 00000BB7h
00000216    93 42   cmp     r3, r2
00000218    12 d9   bls     LAB_00000240
0000021a    0d 4b   ldr     r3, [DAT_00000250]      = 41004400h
```

```
0000021c        19 69   ldr     r1, [r3, #offset DAT_41004410]
0000021e        80 22   mov     r2, #0x80
00000220        52 03   lsl     r2, r2, #0xd
00000222        0a 43   orr     r2, r1
00000224        1a 61   str     r2, [r3, #offset DAT_41004410]
00000226        0c 48   ldr     r0, [LAB_00000256+2]
        LAB_00000228                    XREF[1]:    0000022c(j)
00000228        01 38   sub     r0, #0x1
0000022a        00 28   cmp     r0, #0x0
0000022c        fc dc   bgt     LAB_00000228
0000022e        0b 48   ldr     r0, [LAB_0000025c]
00000230        01 68   ldr     r1, [r0, #0x0]
00000232        02 22   mov     r2, #0x2
00000234        91 43   bic     r1, r2
00000236        01 60   str     r1, [r0, #0x0]
00000238        1a 69   ldr     r2, [r3, #offset DAT_41004410]
0000023a        06 49   ldr     r1, [DAT_00000254]         = FFh
0000023c        0a 40   and     r2, r1
0000023e        1a 61   str     r2, [r3, #offset DAT_41004410]
        LAB_00000240                    XREF[1]:    00000218(j)
00000240        70 47   bx      lr
```

In this code, take a look at the following sequence (**Listing 24**).

Listing 24.

```
00000204        0f 4b   ldr     r3, [DAT_00000244]      = 42003000h
00000206        9a 7b   ldrb    r2, [r3, #offset DAT_4200300e]
00000208        3b 22   mov     r2, #0x3b
0000020a        9a 73   strb    r2, [r3, #offset DAT_4200300e]
```

This sequence clears the flags in the Interrupt Flag Status and Clear (INTFLAG) register (address 0x4200300e = 0x42003000 + 0xe) of timer TC4 of ATSAMD21G18 MCU. It seems reasonable to assume that the code in **Listing 23** is nothing else but the Interrupt Handler for Timer TC4.

In this disassembly, we also have the fragments that perform write operations on PORTA using the OUT register (address 0x41004410). Further analyzing shows that the code in **Listing 23** is exactly what we need.
What we also need is to find the code that implements the delay of 3000 mS. The best candidate is the fragment of the disassembly shown in **Listing 25**.

Listing 25.

```
0000020c    0e 4a   ldr    r2, [DAT_00000248]      = 20000024h
0000020e    13 68   ldr    r3, [r2, #0x0] =>DAT_20000024
00000210    59 1c   add    r1, r3, #0x1
00000212    11 60   str    r1, [r2, #0x0] =>DAT_20000024
00000214    0d 4a   ldr    r2, [DAT_0000024c]      = 00000BB7h
00000216    93 42   cmp    r3, r2
00000218    12 d9   bls    LAB_00000240
```

Here, the value 00000BB7h (=2999) is loaded into the core register **r2** and then compared with the value held in register **r3**. From this code fragment, it seems reasonable to assume that the memory block with label **DAT_20000024** contains the counter being incremented by 1 each time the TC4 interrupt is triggered.
While the counter < 3000, no write operation on PORTA is performed. In this case, instruction

```
bls     LAB_00000240
```

branches to

```
bx      lr
```

If the counter reaches 3000, pin **PA20** is set. From this code fragment, it is easily to assume that the value 2999 (=3000 - 1) defines the interval of 3000 mS. This value also hints that timer TC4 overflows every 1 mS.

PA20 stays HIGH during the small delay implemented by the following sequence (**Listing 26**).

Listing 26.

```
00000226        0c 48   ldr     r0, [LAB_00000256+2]
        LAB_00000228                    XREF[1]:    0000022c(j)
00000228        01 38   sub     r0, #0x1
0000022a        00 28   cmp     r0, #0x0
0000022c        fc dc   bgt     LAB_00000228
```

Then pin **PA20** is reset (=LOW) again.
At this point, we know how the code works, therefore we can patch the binary. Recall that we need to increase the interval before setting pin **PA20** from 3000 mS to 7200 mS.

Patching a HEX file

To change the interval, we first move to the memory block labeled **DAT_0000024c**. The block (**Fig.61**) contains the value 00000BB7h (=2999) that we change to 000001C1F (=7199) (**Fig.62**).

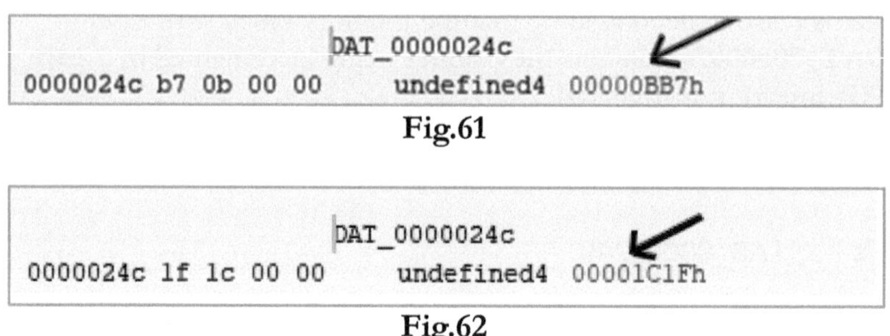

```
                    DAT_0000024c
0000024c b7 0b 00 00        undefined4  00000BB7h
```

Fig.61

```
                    DAT_0000024c
0000024c 1f 1c 00 00        undefined4  00001C1Fh
```

Fig.62

Save the changes and export the modified binary to the HEX file by invoking **File→ Export Program...**. This file can be downloaded into the MCU flash memory.

Example 4

An existing ATSAMD21G18-based embedded system produces the PWM signal with a base frequency of 100 Hz and duty cycle = 80% on pin **PA16**. The PWM signal is enabled only at the LOW level applied to pin **PA09**. When the signal level on **PA09** goes HIGH, the PWM signal is disabled.

This is illustrated in **Fig.63** - **Fig.64**.

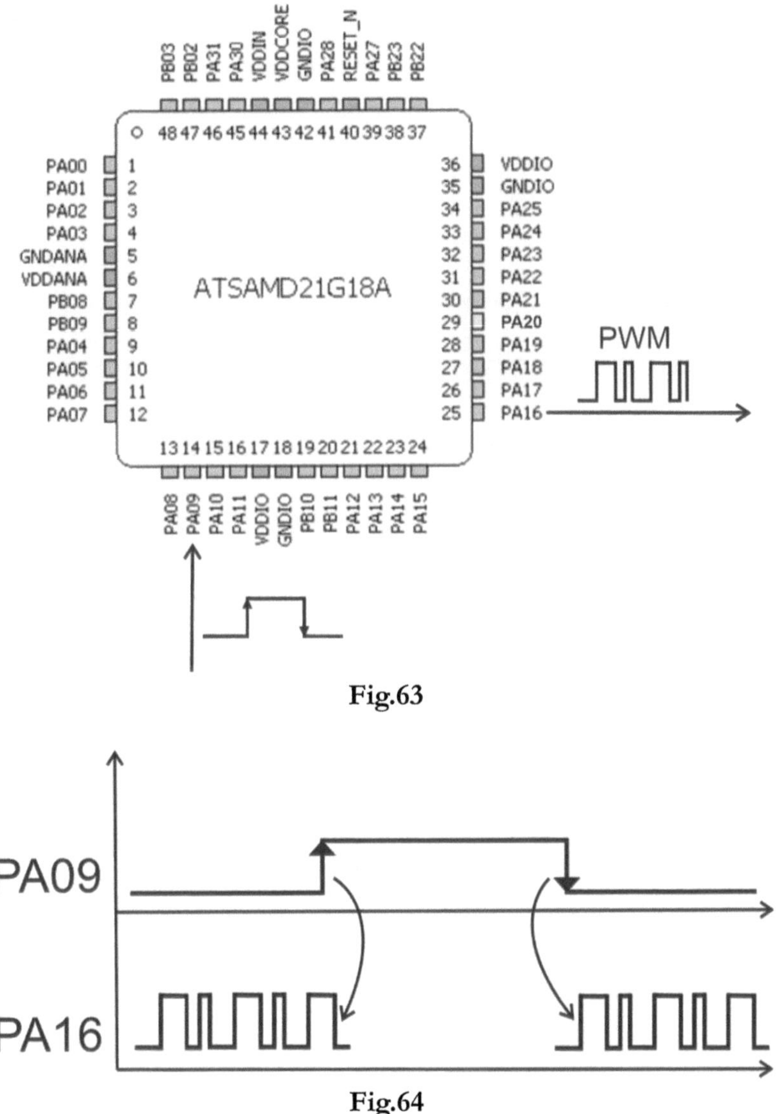

Fig.63

Fig.64

We need to modify the embedded code so that a HIGH level on pin **PA09** will force the PWM duty cycle to reduce to 50% as is illustrated in **Fig.65**.

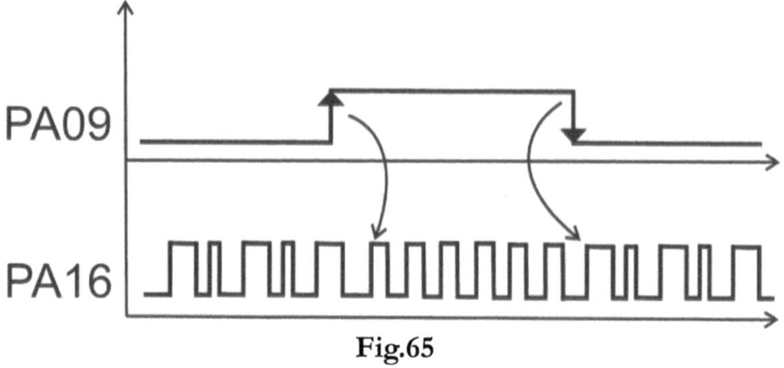

Fig.65

Analyzing a binary

First, we analyze the binary file (named **demo4.hex**) using the GHIDRA Disassembler. To begin, we create the GHIDRA project, then import **demo4.hex** and select ARM:v8:LE:32:default language (**Fig.66**).

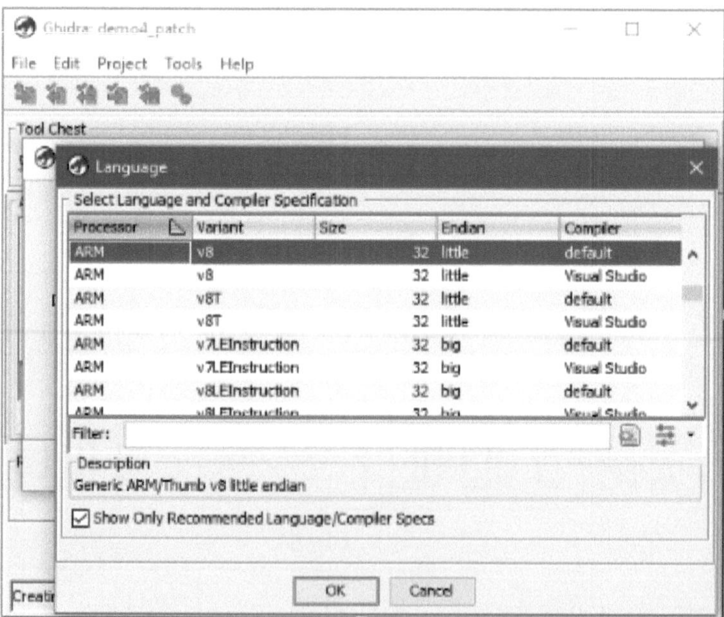

Fig.66

After GHIDRA has generated the disassembly, we will search for the **main()** function. In this particular case, the best candidate for **main()** is function **FUN_000002e4** whose decompile code is shown in **Listing 27**.

Listing 27.

```
void FUN_000002e4(void)
{
 int *piVar1;
 FUN_00000464(0);
 FUN_00000508();
 FUN_00000208();
 FUN_00000520(9);
 FUN_000003c8();
 FUN_000004b4();
 piVar1 = DAT_00000334;
 do {
  do {
   while (*piVar1 == 1) {
    FUN_000004d0();
    *DAT_00000334 = 0;
   }
  } while (*piVar1 != 2);
  FUN_000004b4();
  FUN_000004ec(8000);
  *piVar1 = 0;
 } while( true );
}
```

For convenience, rename **FUN_000002e4** to **main** and save changes. The disassembly of **main()** is shown in **Listing 28**.

Listing 28.

```
***********************************************************
*                        FUNCTION                         *
*************************************** *************
              undefined main(void)
```

```
                    assume LRset = 0x0
                    assume TMode = 0x1
        undefined       r0:1        <RETURN>
                   main                          XREF[1]:    000002c0(c)
000002e4        70 b5           push    { r4, r5, r6, lr }
000002e6        00 20           mov     r0, #0x0
000002e8        00 f0 bc f8     bl      FUN_00000464
000002ec        00 f0 0c f9     bl      FUN_00000508
000002f0        ff f7 8a ff     bl      FUN_00000208
000002f4        09 20           mov     r0, #0x9
000002f6        00 f0 13 f9     bl      FUN_00000520
000002fa        00 f0 65 f8     bl      FUN_000003c8
000002fe        00 f0 d9 f8     bl      FUN_000004b4
00000302        0c 4c           ldr     r4, [DAT_00000334]
00000304        25 00           mov     r5, r4
00000306        26 00           mov     r6, r4
00000308        04 e0           b       LAB_00000314
              LAB_0000030a                       XREF[1]:    00000318(j)
0000030a        00 f0 e1 f8     bl      FUN_000004d0
0000030e        00 22           mov     r2, #0x0
00000310        08 4b           ldr     r3, [DAT_00000334]
00000312        1a 60           str     r2, [r3, #0x0]
              LAB_00000314          XREF[3]:    00000308(j), 0000031e(j),
                                                00000330(j)
00000314        23 68           ldr     r3, [r4, #0x0]
00000316        01 2b           cmp     r3, #0x1
00000318        f7 d0           beq     LAB_0000030a
0000031a        2b 68           ldr     r3, [r5, #0x0]
0000031c        02 2b           cmp     r3, #0x2
0000031e        f9 d1           bne     LAB_00000314
00000320        00 f0 c8 f8     bl      FUN_000004b4
00000324        fa 20           mov     r0, #0xfa
00000326        40 01           lsl     r0, r0, #0x5
00000328        00 f0 e0 f8     bl      FUN_000004ec
0000032c        00 23           mov     r3, #0x0
0000032e        33 60           str     r3, [r6, #0x0]
00000330        f0 e7           b       LAB_00000314
```

Obviously, we need to write some patch that changes the parameters of a PWM signal. For that reason, we should know what timer produces PWM. Since the SAMD21G18 timers are assigned the addresses beginning from **4200**, we begin to search for the string **4200** (**Fig.67**) within the disassembly.

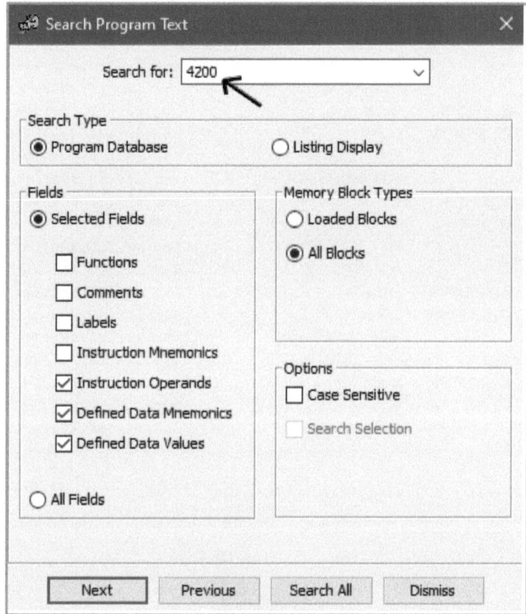

Fig.67

This gives us the following table (**Fig.68**).

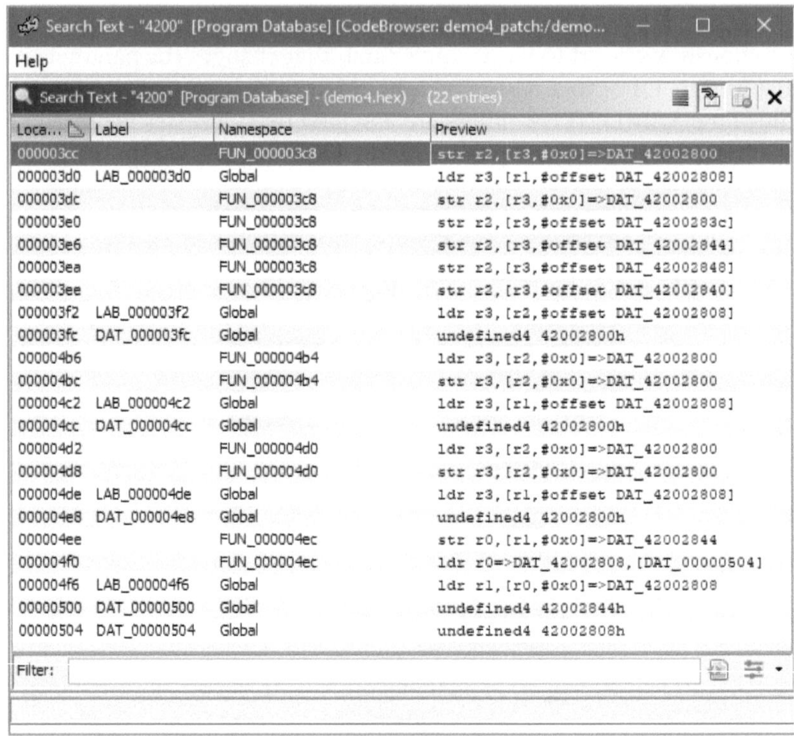

Loca...	Label	Namespace	Preview
000003cc		FUN_000003c8	str r2,[r3,#0x0]=>DAT_42002800
000003d0	LAB_000003d0	Global	ldr r3,[r1,#offset DAT_42002808]
000003dc		FUN_000003c8	str r2,[r3,#0x0]=>DAT_42002800
000003e0		FUN_000003c8	str r2,[r3,#offset DAT_4200283c]
000003e6		FUN_000003c8	str r2,[r3,#offset DAT_42002844]
000003ea		FUN_000003c8	str r2,[r3,#offset DAT_42002848]
000003ee		FUN_000003c8	str r2,[r3,#offset DAT_42002840]
000003f2	LAB_000003f2	Global	ldr r3,[r2,#offset DAT_42002808]
000003fc	DAT_000003fc	Global	undefined4 42002800h
000004b6		FUN_000004b4	ldr r3,[r2,#0x0]=>DAT_42002800
000004bc		FUN_000004b4	str r3,[r2,#0x0]=>DAT_42002800
000004c2	LAB_000004c2	Global	ldr r3,[r1,#offset DAT_42002808]
000004cc	DAT_000004cc	Global	undefined4 42002800h
000004d2		FUN_000004d0	ldr r3,[r2,#0x0]=>DAT_42002800
000004d8		FUN_000004d0	str r3,[r2,#0x0]=>DAT_42002800
000004de	LAB_000004de	Global	ldr r3,[r1,#offset DAT_42002808]
000004e8	DAT_000004e8	Global	undefined4 42002800h
000004ee		FUN_000004ec	str r0,[r1,#0x0]=>DAT_42002844
000004f0		FUN_000004ec	ldr r0=>DAT_42002808,[DAT_00000504]
000004f6	LAB_000004f6	Global	ldr r1,[r0,#0x0]=>DAT_42002808
00000500	DAT_00000500	Global	undefined4 42002844h
00000504	DAT_00000504	Global	undefined4 42002808h

Fig.68

As it is seen from **Fig.68**, the application operates with timer TCC2 whose base address is 0x42002800. It is also seen that the PWM signal is produced by Channel 0 of TCC2 (address 0x42002844) on pin **PA16**.
Further analyzing the disassembly of **main()** (see **Listing 28**) shows that the code fragment

```
000002e8    00 f0 bc f8    bl     FUN_00000464
000002ec    00 f0 0c f9    bl     FUN_00000508
000002f0    ff f7 8a ff    bl     FUN_00000208
000002f4    09 20          mov    r0, #0x9
000002f6    00 f0 13 f9    bl     FUN_00000520
```

performs the initialization of the I/O pins and External Interrupt Controller (EIC). Particularly, line 9 of EIC is configured to trigger an interrupt on both rising and falling edges on pin **PA09**.

Function **FUN_000003c8** performs the initialization of TCC2 Channel 0 and **FUN_000004b4** starts timer TCC2. For convenience, rename **FUN_000003c8** to **pwm_init** and **FUN_000004b4** to **pwm_start**.

One more function that we need to analyze is **FUN_000004ec** - its disassembly is shown in **Listing 29**.

Listing 29.

```
*************************************************************
*                         FUNCTION                          *
*************************************************************
              undefined FUN_000004ec()
               assume LRset = 0x0
               assume TMode = 0x1
      undefined       r0:1        <RETURN>
              FUN_000004ec              XREF[1]:   main:00000328(c)
000004ec      04 49   ldr    r1, [DAT_00000500]        = 42002844h
000004ee      08 60   str    r0, [r1, #0x0] =>DAT_42002844
000004f0      04 48   ldr    r0 =>DAT_42002808, [DAT_00000504]
= 42002808h
000004f2      01 22   mov    r2, #0x1
000004f4      12 02   lsl    r2, r2, #0x8
           LAB_000004f6                 XREF[1]:   000004fc(j)
000004f6      01 68   ldr    r1, [r0, #0x0] =>DAT_42002808
000004f8      11 40   and    r1, r2
000004fa      00 29   cmp    r1, #0x0
000004fc      fb d1   bne    LAB_000004f6
000004fe      70 47   bx     lr
```

To better understand what **FUN_000004ec** does, we should take a look at the following fragment from **Listing 28**:

```
00000324      fa 20          mov    r0, #0xfa
00000326      40 01          lsl    r0, r0, #0x5
00000328      00 f0 e0 f8    bl     FUN_000004ec
```

The above sequence loads a value 0x1f40 (= 8000) into the core register **r0**, then calls function **FUN_000004ec**. Therefore, it seems reasonable to assume that **FUN_000004ec** takes a single parameter in register **r0**.

Further analyzing shows that function **FUN_000004ec** writes the value passed in register **r0** into the memory-mapped address 0x42002844 (= 0x42002800 + 0x44). The address 0x42002844 is assigned to the Compare/Capture Channel 0 register of timer TCC2 (TCC2_CC0). In this configuration, the TCC2_CC0 register contains the value that defines the pulse width of the PWM signal.
The following sequence from **Listing 29** writes the value 8000 into register TCC2_CC0:

```
000004ec        04 49   ldr      r1, [DAT_00000500]          = 42002844h
000004ee        08 60   str      r0, [r1, #0x0] =>DAT_42002844
```

The rest of the code of this function performs the synchronization of timer after writing data into TCC2_CC0.

For convenience, rename **FUN_000004ec** to **set_pulse**. Also rename the memory block labeled **DAT_00000500** to **TCC2_CC0**.
One more interesting function from **Listing 28** is **FUN_000004d0**. Its disassembly is shown in **Listing 30**.

Listing 30.

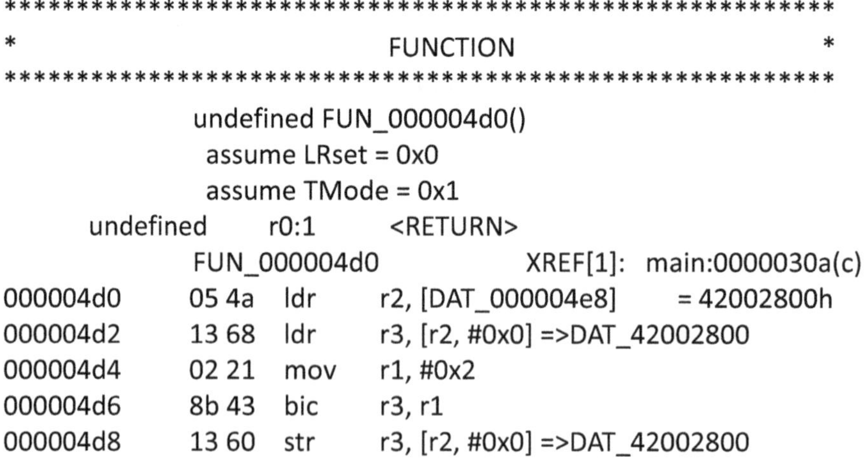

```
**************************************************************
*                          FUNCTION                          *
**************************************************************
                  undefined FUN_000004d0()
                   assume LRset = 0x0
                   assume TMode = 0x1
          undefined       r0:1         <RETURN>
                  FUN_000004d0                    XREF[1]:   main:0000030a(c)
000004d0        05 4a   ldr      r2, [DAT_000004e8]        = 42002800h
000004d2        13 68   ldr      r3, [r2, #0x0] =>DAT_42002800
000004d4        02 21   mov      r1, #0x2
000004d6        8b 43   bic      r3, r1
000004d8        13 60   str      r3, [r2, #0x0] =>DAT_42002800
```

```
000004da        11 00   mov     r1, r2
000004dc        02 22   mov     r2, #0x2
                LAB_000004de                    XREF[1]:    000004e2(j)
000004de        8b 68   ldr     r3, [r1, #offset DAT_42002808]
000004e0        1a 42   tst     r2, r3
000004e2        fc d1   bne     LAB_000004de
000004e4        70 47   bx      lr
```

The first 5 lines of disassembly illustrates what this function does. The code first loads the content of the TCC2 Control A register (TCC2_CTRLA) into the core register **r3** by the sequence

```
000004d0        05 4a   ldr     r2, [DAT_000004e8]          = 42002800h
000004d2        13 68   ldr     r3, [r2, #0x0] =>DAT_42002800
```

Then the sequence

```
000004d4        02 21   mov     r1, #0x2
000004d6        8b 43   bic     r3, r1
000004d8        13 60   str     r3, [r2, #0x0] =>DAT_42002800
```

clears bit 2 in register **r3** and writes the data in **r3** back into the register TCC2_CTRLA. Bit 2 in TCC2_CTRLA enables/disables timer TCC2. In our case, bit 2 = 0, therefore timer TCC2 will be disabled after the write operation is complete. For convenience, rename **FUN_000004d0** to **pwm_stop** and **DAT_000004e8** to **TCC2_CTRLA**. The rest of code of this function performs the synchronizations of peripherals after the write operation.

The disassembly from **Listing 28** also contains a few **cmp** instructions that operate with some variable associated with label **DAT_00000334**. It seems reasonable to assume that the value of this variable determines when to enable /disable PWM.

After saving all changes, the updated version of **Listing 27** will look like the following (**Listing 31**):

Listing 31.

```
void main(void)
{
 int *piVar1;
 FUN_00000464(0);
 FUN_00000508();
 FUN_00000208();
 FUN_00000520(9);
 pwm_init();
 pwm_start();
 piVar1 = DAT_00000334;
 do {
  do {
   while (*piVar1 == 1) {
    pwm_stop();
    *DAT_00000334 = 0;
   }
  } while (*piVar1 != 2);
  pwm_start();
  set_pulse();
  *piVar1 = 0;
 } while( true );
}
```

Although the decompiled code from the above listing looks a bit odd, this gives us the understanding of how the **main()** code works. From this code, it is seen that generating PWM is disabled when variable pointed by **piVar1** becomes = 1. Conversely, PWM is enabled when the variable pointed by **piVar1** = 2.

The updated disassembly of the **main()** function is shown in **Listing 32**. It is seen that the pointers **piVar1** and **DAT_000000334** refer to the same address, **200000DCh**.

Listing 32.

```
*******************************************************
*                      FUNCTION                       *
*******************************************************
```

```
                    undefined main(void)
                      assume LRset = 0x0
                      assume TMode = 0x1
          undefined        r0:1        <RETURN>
                    main                          XREF[1]:    000002c0(c)
000002e4      70 b5           push     { r4, r5, r6, lr }
000002e6      00 20           mov r0, #0x0
000002e8      00 f0 bc f8     bl       FUN_00000464
000002ec      00 f0 0c f9     bl       FUN_00000508
000002f0      ff f7 8a ff     bl       FUN_00000208
000002f4      09 20           mov      r0, #0x9
000002f6      00 f0 13 f9     bl       FUN_00000520
000002fa      00 f0 65 f8     bl       pwm_init
000002fe      00 f0 d9 f8     bl       pwm_start
00000302      0c 4c           ldr      r4, [DAT_00000334] =
                                                          200000DCh
00000304      25 00           mov      r5, r4
00000306      26 00           mov      r6, r4
00000308      04 e0           b        LAB_00000314
                    LAB_0000030a                  XREF[1]:    00000318(j)
0000030a      00 f0 e1 f8     bl       pwm_stop
0000030e      00 22           mov      r2, #0x0
00000310      08 4b           ldr      r3, [DAT_00000334]  =
                                                          200000DCh
00000312      1a 60           str      r2, [r3, #0x0] =>DAT_200000dc
                    LAB_00000314              XREF[3]:    00000308(j),
                                                          0000031e(j),
                                                          00000330(j)
00000314      23 68           ldr      r3, [r4, #0x0] =>DAT_200000dc
00000316      01 2b           cmp      r3, #0x1
00000318      f7 d0           beq      LAB_0000030a
0000031a      2b 68           ldr      r3, [r5, #0x0] =>DAT_200000dc
0000031c      02 2b           cmp      r3, #0x2
0000031e      f9 d1           bne      LAB_00000314
00000320      00 f0 c8 f8     bl       pwm_start
00000324      fa 20           mov      r0, #0xfa
00000326      40 01           lsl      r0, r0, #0x5
```

```
00000328        00 f0 e0 f8     bl          set_pulse
0000032c        00 23           mov         r3, #0x0
0000032e        33 60           str         r3, [r6, #0x0] =>DAT_200000dc
00000330        f0 e7           b           LAB_00000314
00000332        c0 46           mov         r8, r8
                DAT_00000334         XREF[2]:    main:00000302(R),
                                                 main:00000310(R)
00000334        dc 00 00 20     undefined4      200000DCh
```

At this point, one question still remains unanswered: how the data at address **200000DCh** are accessed. It seems reasonable to assume that this can be done by the External Interrupt Handler that is called when the interrupt on line 9 (pin **PA09**) is triggered.

Next, we need to find the disassembly fragment that accesses the data at address **200000DCh**. Traversing the overall code gives us the interesting disassembly that begins at address 00000404 (**Listing 33)**.

Listing 33.

```
00000404        08 4b   ldr     r3, [DAT_00000428]        = 40001800h
00000406        1b 69   ldr     r3, [r3, #offset DAT_40001810]
00000408        08 4b   ldr     r3, [DAT_0000042c]        = 41004400h
0000040a        1b 6a   ldr     r3, [r3, #offset DAT_41004420]
0000040c        9b 05   lsl     r3, r3, #0x16
0000040e        07 d4   bmi     LAB_00000420
00000410        02 22   mov     r2, #0x2
00000412        07 4b   ldr     r3, [DAT_00000430]     = 200000DCh
00000414        1a 60   str     r2, [r3, #0x0] =>DAT_200000dc
            LAB_00000416
00000416        80 22   mov     r2, #0x80
00000418        92 00   lsl     r2, r2, #0x2
0000041a        03 4b   ldr     r3, [DAT_00000428]        = 40001800h
0000041c        1a 61   str     r2, [r3, #offset DAT_40001810]
0000041e        70 47   bx      lr
            LAB_00000420
00000420        01 22   mov     r2, #0x1
00000422        03 4b   ldr     r3, [DAT_00000430]    = 200000DCh
00000424        1a 60   str     r2, [r3, #0x0] =>DAT_200000dc
```

```
00000426        f6 e7   b       LAB_00000416
             DAT_00000428
00000428        00 18 00 40     undefined4      40001800h
             DAT_0000042c
0000042c        00 44 00 41     undefined4      41004400h
```

In this disassembly, the sequence

```
00000408        08 4b   ldr     r3, [DAT_0000042c]       = 41004400h
0000040a        1b 6a   ldr     r3, [r3, #offset DAT_41004420]
```

reads data from PORTA. Then all data bits are left-shifted by 22 positions by the instruction

```
0000040c        9b 05   lsl     r3, r3, #0x16
```

The next instruction tests bit 9 of PORTA (pin **PA09**):

```
0000040e        07 d4   bmi     LAB_00000420
```

If bit 9 = 1, the **bmi** instruction branches to label **LAB_00000420**. The code fragment that runs at this label writes 1 into address **200000DCh**.

If bit 9 = 0, the **bmi** instruction is skipped and the sequence

```
00000410        02 22   mov     r2, #0x2
00000412        07 4b   ldr     r3, [DAT_00000430]      = 200000DCh
00000414        1a 60   str     r2, [r3, #0x0] =>DAT_200000dc
```

writes 2 into address **200000DCh.**
At this point, we have the code that writes the data to address 200000DCh. Recall that the value held at this address is tested by the code within the **main()** function (see **Listing 31** - **Listing 32**) in order to determine whether to enable / disable PWM.
Further traversing the code in **Listing 33** hints that the sequence

```
00000416        80 22   mov     r2, #0x80
00000418        92 00   lsl     r2, r2, #0x2
0000041a        03 4b   ldr     r3, [DAT_00000428]      = 40001800h
```

```
0000041c        1a 61   str     r2, [r3, #offset DAT_40001810]
```

simply clears the interrupt flag EXTINT9 in the Interrupt Flag Status and Clear register (INTFLAG, address 0x40001800 + 0x10) of EIC.
To summarize, the code fragment in **Listing 33** belongs to the Interrupt Handler that processes interrupt triggered on line 9 (pin **PA09**) of EIC.

At this point, we already understand how PWM is controlled, therefore we can try to patch the binary.

Patching a HEX file

After analyzing the disassembly, it becomes clear that we can patch the code without allocating extra space. We can simply put the patch into the **pwm_stop()** function whose disassembly is shown in **Listing 34**.

Listing 34.

```
**************************************************************
*                          FUNCTION                          *
**************************************************************
                undefined pwm_stop(void)
                 assume LRset = 0x0
                 assume TMode = 0x1
        undefined       r0:1        <RETURN>
                pwm_stop                    XREF[1]:   main:0000030a(c)
000004d0        05 4a   ldr     r2, [TCC2_CTRLA]    = 42002800h
000004d2        13 68   ldr     r3, [r2, #0x0] =>DAT_42002800
000004d4        02 21   mov     r1, #0x2
000004d6        8b 43   bic     r3, r1
000004d8        13 60   str     r3, [r2, #0x0] =>DAT_42002800
000004da        11 00   mov     r1, r2
000004dc        02 22   mov     r2, #0x2
              LAB_000004de                  XREF[1]:   000004e2(j)
000004de        8b 68   ldr     r3, [r1, #offset DAT_42002808]
000004e0        1a 42   tst     r2, r3
000004e2        fc d1   bne     LAB_000004de
```

```
000004e4        70 47    bx        lr
```

Additionally, the code in the **Decompiler** window (**Listing 35**) helps us to better understand what the **pwm_stop()** code does.

Listing 35.

```
void pwm_stop(void)
{
  uint *puVar1;
  puVar1 = TCC2_CTRLA;
  *TCC2_CTRLA = *TCC2_CTRLA & 0xfffffffd;
  do {
  } while ((puVar1[2] & 2) != 0);
  return;
}
```

The following sequence from **Listing 34**

```
000004d0        05 4a    ldr       r2, [TCC2_CTRLA]    = 42002800h
000004d2        13 68    ldr       r3, [r2, #0x0] =>DAT_42002800
000004d4        02 21    mov       r1, #0x2
000004d6        8b 43    bic       r3, r1
000004d8        13 60    str       r3, [r2, #0x0] =>DAT_42002800
```

simply disables timer TCC2 by clearing the ENABLE bit (bit 1 in register TCC2_CTRLA) using instruction **bic**. For convenience, we assign the label **TCC2_CTRLA** to the address 0x42002800h.
The code fragment

```
                LAB_000004de                XREF[1]:    000004e2(j)
000004de        8b 68    ldr       r3, [r1, #offset DAT_42002808]
000004e0        1a 42    tst       r2, r3
000004e2        fc d1    bne       LAB_000004de
000004e4        70 47    bx        lr
```

performs the synchronization of the peripheral after writing data.

Let's recall what we need to change in this embedded code. Instead of disabling PWM on the TCC2 Channel 0 output at the rising edge on pin **PA09**, we must simply set the PWM duty cycle to 50%.
Since the **pwm_stop()** function is not used elsewhere in this application, we can safely patch the code of this function.

For convenience, let's change a few labels of a few memory blocks relating to timer TCC2 as is shown below:

```
                TCC2_CTRLA        XREF[1]:   pwm_start:000004b4(R)
000004e8        00 28 00 42     undefined4      42002800h
                TCC2_CC0          XREF[2]:   pwm_stop:000004d0(R),
                                             set_pulse:000004ec(R)
00000500        44 28 00 42     undefined4      42002844h
                TCC2_SYNCBUSY     XREF[2]:   pwm_stop:000004da(R),
                                             set_pulse:000004f0(R)
00000504        08 28 00 42     undefined4      42002808h
```

After patching the code, function **pwm_stop()** will look like the following (**Listing 36**).

Listing 36.

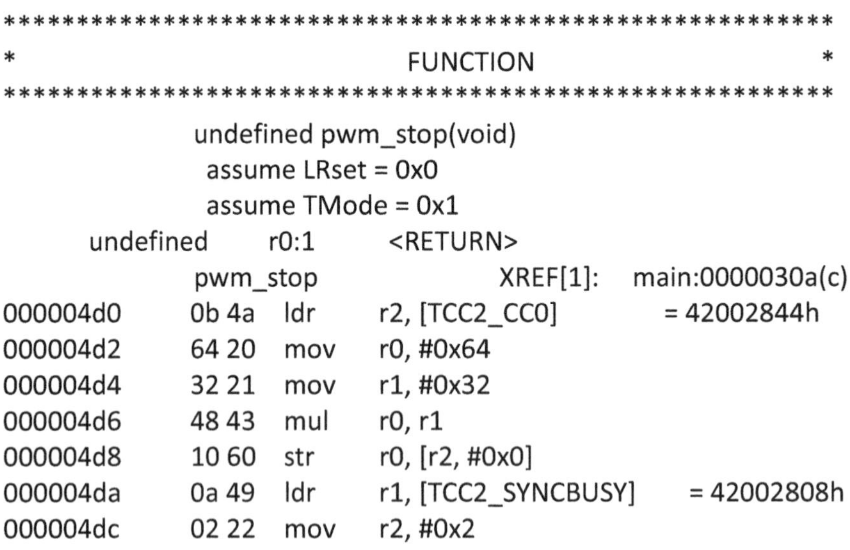

```
**********************************************************
*                        FUNCTION                        *
**********************************************************
                undefined pwm_stop(void)
                 assume LRset = 0x0
                 assume TMode = 0x1
        undefined      r0:1        <RETURN>
                pwm_stop                    XREF[1]:   main:0000030a(c)
000004d0        0b 4a   ldr    r2, [TCC2_CC0]            = 42002844h
000004d2        64 20   mov    r0, #0x64
000004d4        32 21   mov    r1, #0x32
000004d6        48 43   mul    r0, r1
000004d8        10 60   str    r0, [r2, #0x0]
000004da        0a 49   ldr    r1, [TCC2_SYNCBUSY]       = 42002808h
000004dc        02 22   mov    r2, #0x2
```

```
                LAB_000004de                XREF[1]:   000004e2(j)
000004de       0b 68   ldr      r3, [r1, #0x0]
000004e0       1a 42   tst      r2, r3
000004e2       fc d1   bne      LAB_000004de
000004e4       70 47   bx       lr
000004e6       c0      ??       C0h
000004e7       46      ??       46h      F
```

As compared with the original code of function **pwm_stop()** (see **Listing 34**), the code disabling timer TCC2 is replaced by the sequence that writes the new value of pulse width into the register TCC2_CC0. The value of a pulse width (=0x64 x 0x32 = 0x1388 = 5000) is calculated by the sequence

```
000004d2       64 20   mov      r0, #0x64
000004d4       32 21   mov      r1, #0x32
000004d6       48 43   mul      r0, r1
```

The modified code is then exported to the HEX file that can further be downloaded into the MCU flash memory.

Example 5

An existing embedded system based upon ATSAMD21G18A Cortex-M0+ generates the sine wave signal on pin **PA02** with a frequency of 1.5kHz (**Fig.69**).

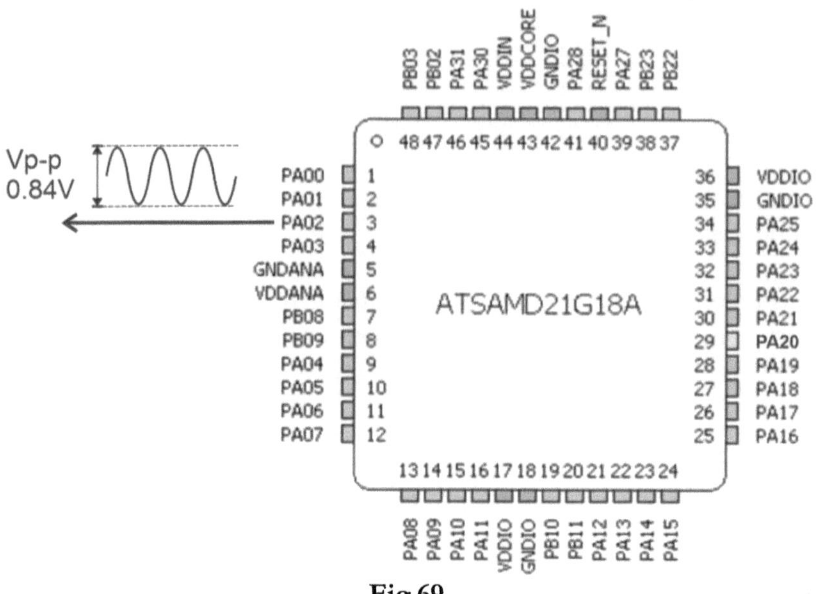

Fig.69

The problem is that the amplitude (a peak-to-peak voltage, **Vp-p**) of a signal is insufficient to drive the external mixed-signal circuitry. In this particular case, **Vp-p** ≈ 0.84V (**Fig.70**).

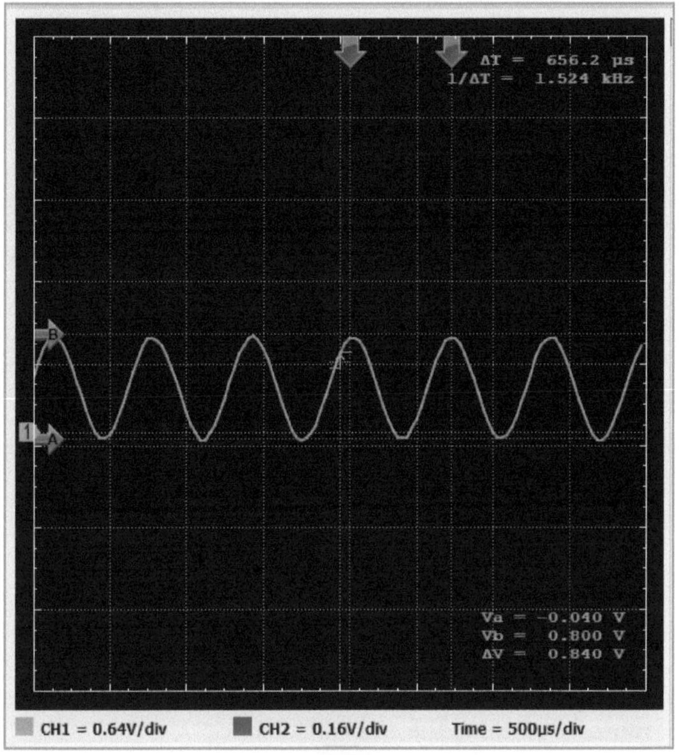

Fig.70

The external circuitry, meanwhile, requires the amplitude at least 1.7V at its input (**Fig.71**).

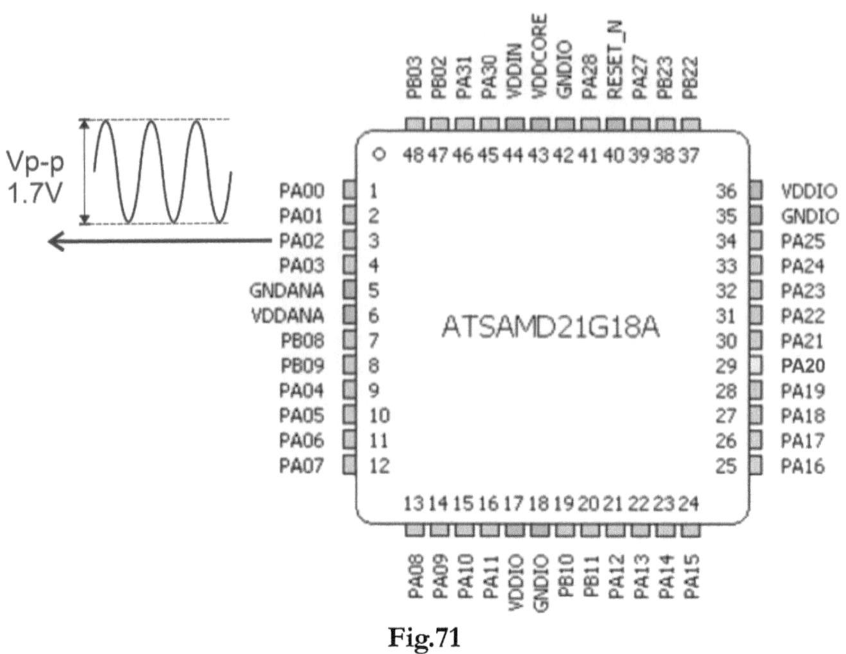

Fig.71

To solve the problem, we must increase the amplitude of a sine wave more than 2 times by patching the embedded code.

Once a microcontroller generates a sinewave signal on pin **PA02**, it means that a Digital-To-Analog Converter (DAC) is used. There should also be some clocking system (usually, a timer) synchronizing DAC.

Analyzing a binary

As usual, we create a new project in the GHIDRA Disassembler and import an original HEX file. To analyze the binary, we will use ARM:v8:LE:32:default assembler.

First, we try to determine where the **main()** code is located. In this particular case, analyzing with default options doesn't give us any functions. Only after choosing **Analysis→Analyze All Open…** (**Fig.72**) and enabling the **ARM Aggressive Instruction Finder (Prototype)** option (**Fig.73**), we finally get the list of functions in the **Symbol Tree** window.

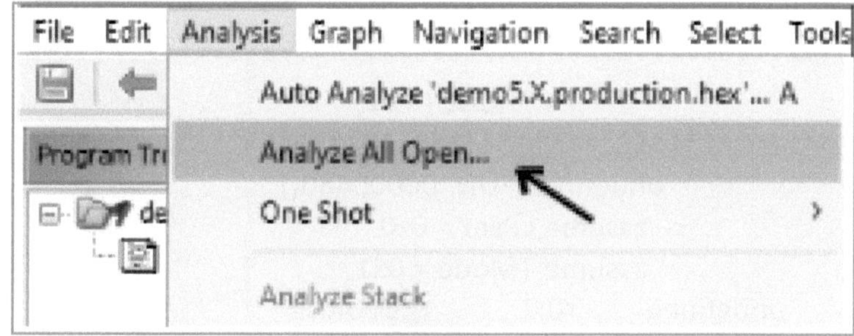

Fig.72

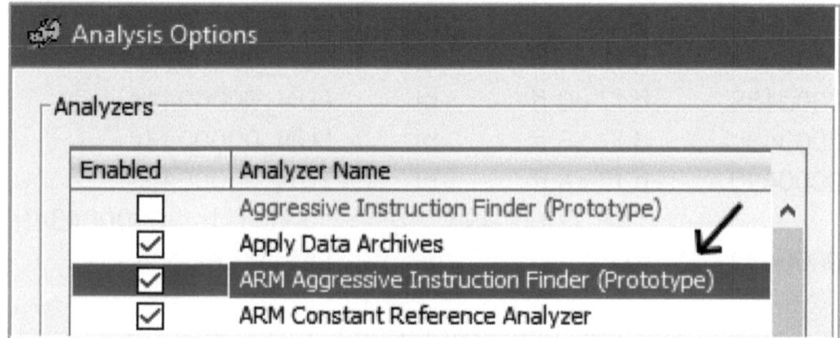

Fig.73

Traversing the functions in **Symbol Tree** gives us the possible candidate for the **main()** that is function **FUN_00000480** (**Listing 37**- **Listing 38**).

Listing 37.

```
void FUN_00000480(void)
{
  FUN_000003fc(0);
  FUN_0000044c();
  FUN_0000033c();
  FUN_00000468();
  do {
                /* WARNING: Do nothing block with infinite loop */
  } while ( true );
}
```

Listing 38.

```
********************************************************
*                          FUNCTION                          *
********************************************************
                    undefined FUN_00000480()
                     assume LRset = 0x0
                     assume TMode = 0x1
        undefined        r0:1          <RETURN>
                    FUN_00000480              XREF[1]:    00000240(c)
00000480            10 b5           push     { r4, lr }
00000482            00 20           mov      r0, #0x0
00000484            ff f7 ba ff     bl       FUN_000003fc
00000488            ff f7 e0 ff     bl       FUN_0000044c
0000048c            ff f7 56 ff     bl       FUN_0000033c
00000490            ff f7 ea ff     bl       FUN_00000468
                    LAB_00000494              XREF[1]:    00000494(j)
00000494            fe e7           b        LAB_00000494
```

The above disassembly hints that the code fragments(s) producing the sine wave signal on pin **PA02** is not placed in the **while()** loop of **FUN_00000480**. Obviously, generating a periodical signal is not implemented by **FUN_000003fc**, **FUN_0000044c**, **FUN_0000033** or **FUN_00000468** because these functions are executed only once. It seems reasonable to assume that these functions implement some initialization operations.

For convenience, rename **FUN_00000480** to **main**() and continue analyzing the disassembly.

At this point, we can assume that the code producing a sine wave may be placed within some timer interrupt handler. What we certainly know is that the binary code (sample) of an analog signal must be put into the DATA register of DAC (address 0x42004808 = 0x42004800 + 0x8). The DATA register contains the 10-bit value that is converted to an analog signal by the DAC.

Let's search for all references to the DAC registers beginning from the base address of DAC (=0x42004800) (**Fig.74**).

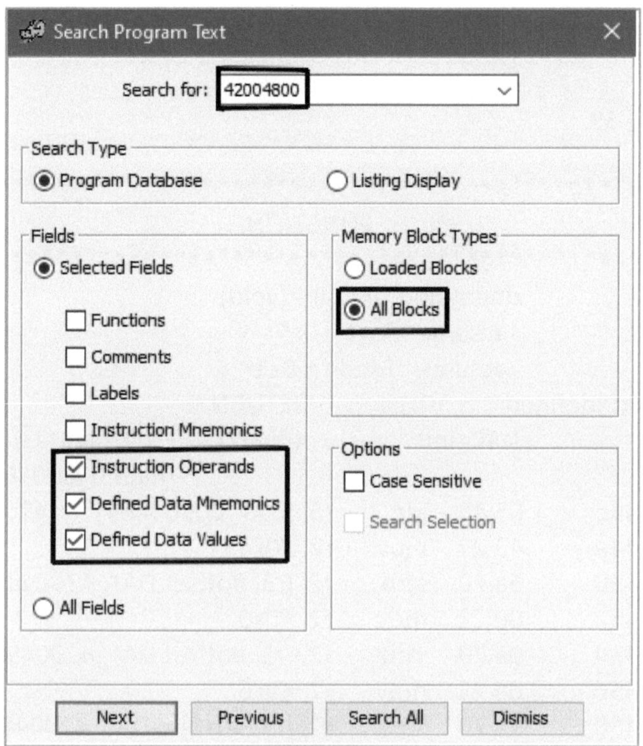

Fig.74

The search returns the following results (**Fig.75**).

Search Text - "42004800" [Program Database] - (demo5.X.production.hex) (2 entries)

Location	Label	Namespace	Preview
00000458		FUN_0000044c	strb r2,[r3,#0x0]=>DAT_42004800
00000464	DAT_00000464	Global	undefined4 42004800h

Filter:

Fig.75

It is seen that function **FUN_0000044c** writes some data into the DAC Control A (CTRLA) register. Therefore, we can assume that this function provides some initialization of the D/A converter. For convenience, rename

FUN_0000044c to **DAC_Init**. The disassembly of this function (**Listing 39**) proves that its code performs configuring DAC.

Listing 39.

```
**************************************************************
*                          FUNCTION                          *
**************************************************************
                  undefined DAC_Init(void)
                   assume LRset = 0x0
                   assume TMode = 0x1
        undefined       r0:1        <RETURN>
                  DAC_Init             XREF[2]:   FUN_000003fc:00000414(c),
                                                  main:00000488(c)
0000044c      05 4b   ldr     r3, [DAT_00000464]   = 42004800h
0000044e      43 22   mov     r2, #0x43
00000450      5a 70   strb    r2, [r3, #offset DAT_42004801]
00000452      00 22   mov     r2, #0x0
00000454      9a 70   strb    r2, [r3, #offset DAT_42004802]
00000456      06 22   mov     r2, #0x6
00000458      1a 70   strb    r2, [r3, #0x0]=>DAT_42004800
0000045a      1a 00   mov     r2, r3
                  LAB_0000045c                XREF[1]:    00000460(j)
0000045c      d3 79   ldrb    r3, [r2, #offset DAT_42004807]
0000045e      00 2b   cmp     r3, #0x0
00000460      fc d1   bne     LAB_0000045c
00000462      70 47   bx      lr
                DAT_00000464          XREF[1]:   DAC_Init:0000044c(R)
00000464      00 48 00 42     undefined4      42004800h
```

The high-level code (**Listing 40**) provided by the GHIDRA Decompiler helps us to better understand how the DAC parameters are configured.

Listing 40.

```
void DAC_Init(void)
{
  undefined *puVar1;
```

```
  puVar1 = DAT_00000464;
  DAT_00000464[1] = 0x43;
  puVar1[2] = 0;
  *puVar1 = 6;
  do {
  } while (puVar1[7] != '\0');
  return;
}
```

Next to search is 0x42004808 that is the address of the DAC DATA register. The reference to this address is not found within the initial disassembly, therefore we need to check unidentified memory blocks containing sequences of bytes.

Let's begin disassembling such blocks from the lowest addresses and see what we gain. After a few unsuccessful attempts to gain some reasonable results, we finally gain the disassembly beginning from address 000002ac (**Listing 41**) that looks like what we need.

Listing 41.

```
000002ac    0b 4b   ldr    r3, [DAT_000002dc]     = 42003400h
000002ae    9a 7b   ldrb   r2, [r3, #offset DAT_4200340e]
000002b0    3b 22   mov    r2, #0x3b
000002b2    9a 73   strb   r2, [r3, #offset DAT_4200340e]
000002b4    0a 4a   ldr    r2, [DAT_000002e0]     = 20000028h
000002b6    13 68   ldr    r3, [r2, #0x0] =>DAT_20000028
000002b8    01 33   add    r3, #0x1
000002ba    13 60   str    r3, [r2, #0x0] =>DAT_20000028
000002bc    3f 2b   cmp    r3, #0x3f
000002be    02 dd   ble    LAB_000002c6
000002c0    00 22   mov    r2, #0x0
000002c2    07 4b   ldr    r3, [DAT_000002e0]   = 20000028h
000002c4    1a 60   str    r2, [r3, #0x0] =>DAT_20000028
                LAB_000002c6               XREF[1]:   000002be(j)
000002c6    06 4b   ldr    r3, [DAT_000002e0]   = 20000028h
000002c8    1b 68   ldr    r3, [r3, #0x0] =>DAT_20000028
000002ca    06 4a   ldr    r2, [DAT_000002e4]     = 0000037Ch
```

```
000002cc      d2 5c    ldrb    r2, [r2, r3] =>DAT_0000037c    = 7Fh
000002ce      06 4b    ldr     r3, [DAT_000002e8]      = 20000008h
000002d0      1a 70    strb    r2, [r3, #0x0] =>DAT_20000008
000002d2      06 48    ldr     r0=>DAT_42004808, [DAT_000002ec]
                                                  = 42004808h
000002d4      06 49    ldr     r1, [DAT_000002f0]    20000008h
000002d6      09 68    ldr     r1, [r1, #0x0] =>DAT_20000008
000002d8      01 60    str     r1, [r0, #0x0] =>DAT_42004808
000002da      70 47    bx      lr
              DAT_000002dc         XREF[1]:    000002ac(R)
000002dc      00 34 00 42     undefined4      42003400h
```

What is interesting in the above disassembly are labels DAT_000002dc and DAT_000002ec. The label DAT_000002dc refers to the value 42003400h that is the base address of timer TC5. The label DAT_000002ec is associated with 42004808h that is the address of DAC DATA register.
The sequence

```
000002b0      3b 22    mov     r2, #0x3b
000002b2      9a 73    strb    r2, [r3, #offset DAT_4200340e]
```

simply clears all bits in the Interrupt Flag Status and Clear (INTFLAG) register of timer TC5.

The similar sequence is usually present in the Interrupt Service handlers. Therefore, we can assume that the code in **Listing 41** belongs to the Interrupt Handler processing the TC5 timer interrupt.
From this disassembly, we can also see that the fragment

```
000002d2      06 48    ldr     r0=>DAT_42004808, [DAT_000002ec]
                                                  = 42004808h
000002d4      06 49    ldr     r1, [DAT_000002f0]     20000008h
000002d6      09 68    ldr     r1, [r1, #0x0] =>DAT_20000008
000002d8      01 60    str     r1, [r0, #0x0] =>DAT_42004808
```

writes the data held at the address 0x20000008 into the address 0x42004808 (register DAC DATA).
For convenience, we rename the disassembly shown in **Listing 41** to **TC5_IRQHandler**.

Let's stop at this point and summarize what we have. Obviously, the code fragment in **Listing 41** processes the TC5 interrupt and writes the binary code (sample) to the DAC DATA register. This binary code defines the amplitude of an output signal. Therefore, in order to increase the amplitude of the output sine wave signal, we need to modify the binary code before it goes to the DAC DATA register.
The next section describes how to patch the binary to increase the amplitude of the output signal.

Patching a HEX file

Let's recall what we need to do. The existing embedded code produces the sine wave signal with the amplitude of about 0.84V. We need to modify an embedded code so that the output signal would have the amplitude at least 1.7V. This means that we need to multiply every 10-bit binary code (sample) being written into the DAC DATA register at least by 1.7V/0.84 = 2.024. Writing a patch for multiplying some value by 2.024 may be a very difficult task because Cortex-M0+ doesn't have the floating-point unit. Nevertheless, in this particular case, we can simply multiply the 10-bit binary code by 3 before writing the sample into the DAC DATA register.
Let's do that.
First, we need to decide where to place the patch. In this particular case, the most reasonable way is to expand the existing memory block (pointed by the arrow in the **Memory Map** window, **Fig. 76**).

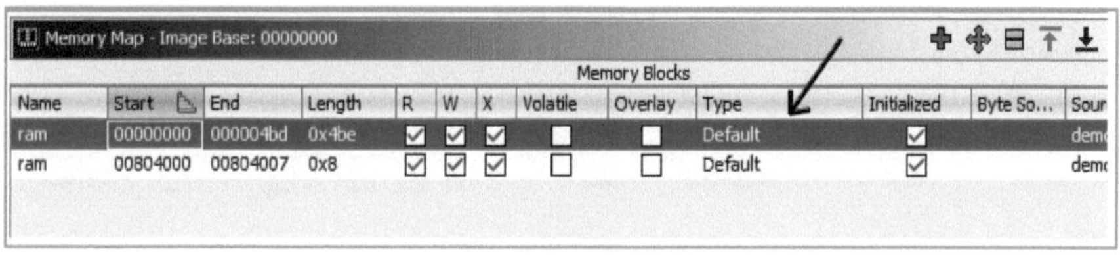
Memory Map - Image Base: 00000000

Memory Blocks

Name	Start	End	Length	R	W	X	Volatile	Overlay	Type	Initialized	Byte So...	Sour
ram	00000000	000004bd	0x4be	☑	☑	☑	☐	☐	Default	☑		dem
ram	00804000	00804007	0x8	☑	☑	☑	☐	☐	Default	☑		dem

Fig.76

This is the memory block where the TC5_IRQHandler code is placed. Since the free space is available for this MCU, we can expand this memory block and place the patch there.
The block starts at address 00000000 and ends at 000004bd. To expand this block, click on the corresponding icon (**Fig.77**).

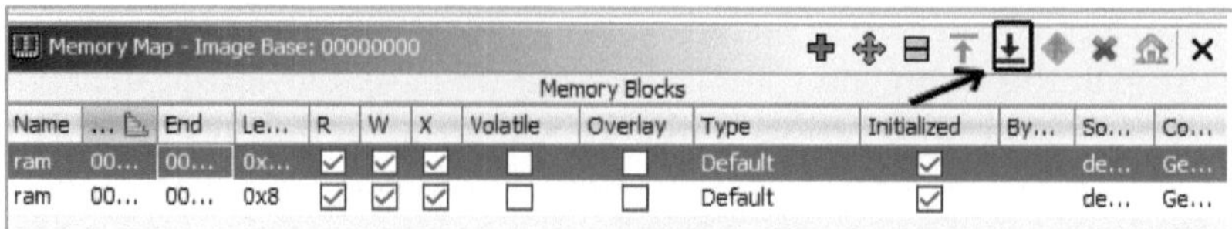

Fig.77

Then type the new end address (**000004cd**, in our case) as is shown in **Fig.78**.

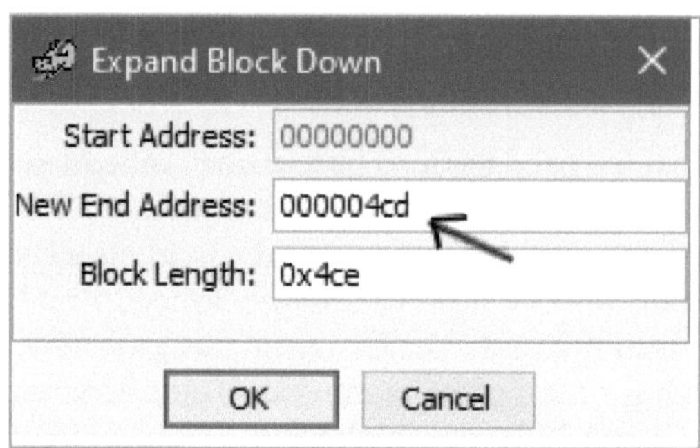

Fig.78

While expanding the memory block, you must always know the exact size (in bytes) of the patch. If the new memory block is less than the size of your patch, you can overwrite the existing code and damage the binary.
In our case, the updated memory map will look like the following (**Fig.79**):

Memory Map - Image Base: 00000000

Name	Start	End	Length	R	W	X	Volatile	Overlay	Type
ram.exp	00000000	000004cd	0x4ce	☑	☑	☑	☐	☐	Default
ram	00804000	00804007	0x8	☑	☑	☑	☐	☐	Default

Fig.79

Now it is time to design a patch. First, we need to insert the branch instruction that will call our patch code. The best place for that is the memory block occupied by the following instructions (see **Listing 41**).

```
000002d8    01 60   str    r1, [r0, #0x0] =>DAT_42004808
000002da    70 47   bx     lr
```

```
                DAT_000002dc      XREF[1]:   000002ac(R)
000002dc        00 34 00 42    undefined4    42003400h
```

We can safely replace both instructions **str** and **bx** with the **bl** instruction that will call our patch placed in the expanded memory area. To summarize, we need to do the following:

1. write the patch in the expanded memory area;
2. rewrite the code within the **TC5_IRQHandler** (**Listing 41**) in order to call the patch.

Let's take step 1.
The patch will begin at the address 000004c0 and will look like the following (**Listing 42**).

Listing 42.

```
            data_correction
000004c0        04 b4   push    { r2 }
000004c2        03 22   mov     r2, #0x3
000004c4        51 43   mul     r1, r2
000004c6        01 60   str     r1, [r0,#0x0]
000004c8        04 bc   pop     { r2 }
000004ca        70 47   bx      lr
```

The above code is simple. The binary code to be written into the DAC DATA register is held in the core register **r1**. The **mul** instruction multiplies this code by 3 and the **str** instruction writes the data in **r1** into the DAC DATA register. This way we get 3 times the amplitude of the output sine wave signal on pin **PA02**.
For convenience, we can create the function from the code in **Listing 42** by right-clicking on the label **data_correction** (**Fig.80**).

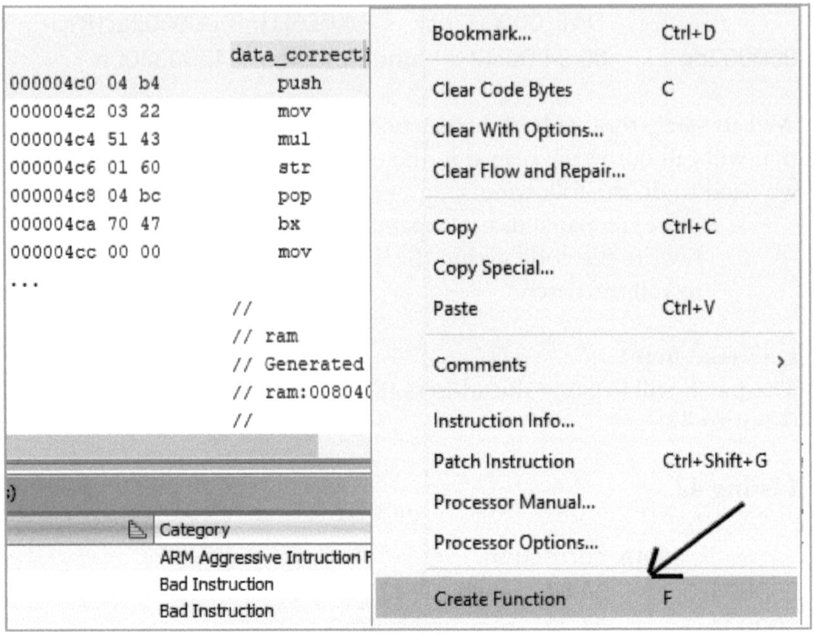

Fig.80

After we are done, the updated listing of the **data_correction()** function will look like the following (**Listing 43**):

Listing 43.

```
**************************************************
*                    FUNCTION                    *
**************************************************
              undefined data_correction()
               assume LRset = 0x0
               assume TMode = 0x1
     undefined      r0:1        <RETURN>
              data_correction
000004c0      04 b4   push    { r2 }
000004c2      03 22   mov     r2, #0x3
000004c4      51 43   mul     r1, r2
000004c6      01 60   str     r1, [r0, #0x0]
000004c8      04 bc   pop     { r2 }
```

```
000004ca        70 47    bx        lr
```

The high-level code for this function produced by the GHIDRA Decompiler will look like the following (**Listing 44**):

Listing 44.

```
void data_correction(int *param_1,int param_2)
{
  *param_1 = param_2 * 3;
  return;
}
```

Notice that **param_1** (passed in register **r0**) in this decompiled code is nothing else but the address of the DAC DATA register. Since we use the core register **r2**, the **Decompiler** interprets that as param_2, although in real life function **data_correction()** doesn't take the 2nd parameter.

Let's take step 2.
Now we need to modify the code within the **TC5_IRQHandler** (**Listing 41**) in order to call **data_correction()**. This modified fragment is shown in **Listing 45.**

Listing 45.

```
000002d8        f2 e0    b         data_correction
000002da        f2       ??        F2h
000002db        f8       ??        F8h
```

Here we replace the instructions **str** and **bx lr** (see **Listing 41**) with a single branch instruction

```
000002d8        f2 e0    b         data_correction
```

that simply passes control to the **data_correction()** function.
When we are done, we can export a full patched code to the HEX file as is described in the previous chapters. Then the HEX file can be downloaded into ATSAMD21G18A flash memory. The sine wave signal produced by the updated embedded code is shown in **Fig.81**.

ΔT = 656.2 µs
1/ΔT = 1.524 kHz
B
1
A
Va = -0.040 V
Vb = 2.400 V
ΔV = 2.440 V
CH1 = 0.64V/div
CH2 = 0.16V/div
Time = 500µs/div

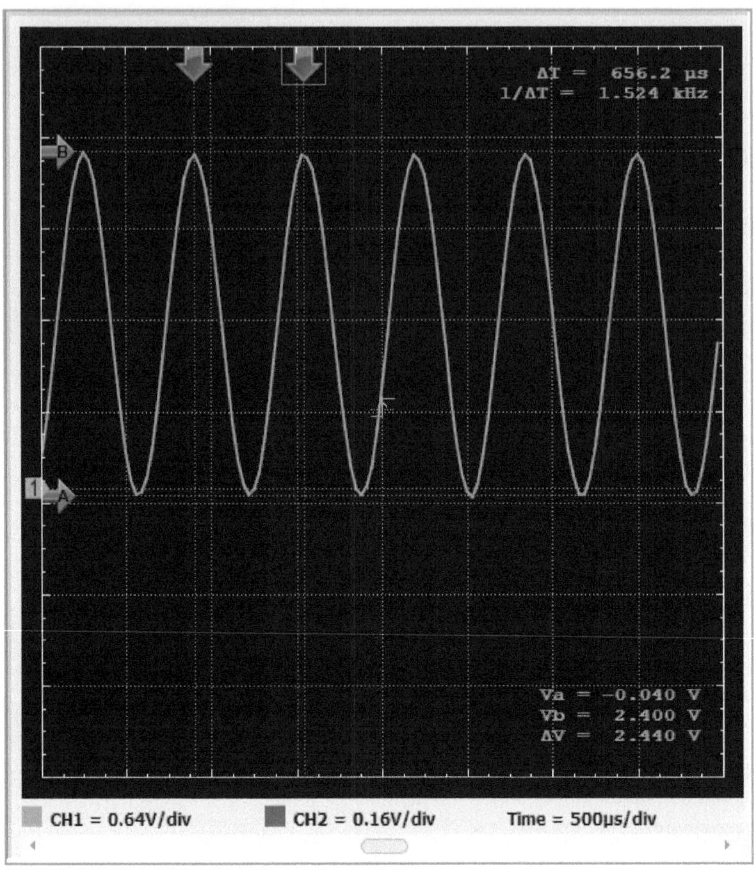

Fig.81

INDEX

Praise for *How to Write Great Dialog*

"As an editor, I wish all my clients would read and apply the advice in this book. James Callan describes the writing of dialog in simple terms ... easy to grasp and apply. He even includes exercises...Highly recommended."
Lorna Collins, multi-published author and content editor

"This book should be in every aspiring writer's library. Writing believable dialog that adds to the storytelling and lets the reader know something about the character is what makes or breaks a novel."
F.M. Meredith: author of Murder in the Worst Degree

"Callan's easy to understand explanations and variety of exercises makes this how-to perfect for the novice, as well as, the seasoned writer."
Michelle J.G. Perin, PSWA Competition Chair, Board Member

"A REALLY HELPFUL book ... will teach you 'everything you need to know about writing dialog,' along with very practical advice..."
Arlene Uslander, author, award-winning journalistic professional editor